THE ODYSSEY OF
SELF-DISCOVERY

THE ODYSSEY OF SELF-DISCOVERY

ON BECOMING A LEADER

XINJIN ZHAO

NEW DEGREE PRESS

THE ODYSSEY OF SELF-DISCOVERY

On Becoming a Leader

ISBN   979-8-88504-460-8 *Paperback*

979-8-88504-484-4 *Ebook*

CONTENTS

INTRODUCTION

Becoming a leader is synonymous with becoming yourself. It is precisely that simple and it is also that difficult.

— WARREN BENNIS

The breeze blowing through a Malawi village in Africa had never turned a windmill until William Kamkwamba, a fourteen-year-old boy, built a wobbly windmill in 2001 from spare parts, including scrap metals, a used tractor fan, a broken bicycle frame, and plastic pipes he scavenged from the village trash. With a copy of an old textbook from the local village library—*Using Energy* with a windmill on the cover—as his only source of information, he was able to create a small miracle that would change the lives around him for the better. He constructed a windmill and generated enough electricity to light his parents' house for the first time (Kamkwamb 2010).

At the time when Kamkwamba was building his windmill, his village was decimated by a deadly famine due to drought. He had to overcome crippling adversity to just get by. Kamkwamba's family lost their seasonal maize crops. His father reduced their meals to once a day and they had to scrounge for food. He had to drop out of school since his parents were no longer able to afford to pay his $80 annual tuition fee.

The adversity did not stop Kamkwamba from pursuing his near-impossible dream: to better his village by bringing electricity and water to it. Kamkwamba went on to build a second windmill a few years later and generated enough electricity to pump water and irrigate his family fields.

He eventually received a scholarship to the African Leadership Academy in South Africa and then received a bachelor's degree in environmental studies from Dartmouth College in the United States. In 2020, he announced the establishment of the Moving Windmills Innovation Center in Kasungu, Malawi: a hands-on, collaborative-learning center designed to inspire the next generation of African Innovators and drive economic prosperity for Malawi (Moving Windmills Project 2022).

William Kamkwamba's story eventually became the bestselling book, *The Boy Who Harnessed The Wind*. It deeply resonated with me who grew up in a remote village in northern China without running water, electricity, or barely enough food. One could credit Kamkwamba's ingenuity or even stubbornness for his original success. However, Kamkwamba could have stopped at one house, or one village. His vision and leadership allowed him to build and pursue a movement out of that one scrappy windmill.

Leadership was not the first word that popped in my head when I first read his book more than ten years ago on a long flight across the Pacific. However, the story of his heroic effort always stayed with me. As I started doing research for my book, I read more about his trajectory fully after his college education.

A fuller picture started to emerge about his early experience and his later pursuit. His early life journey influenced Kamkwamba's leadership and propelled him to take on the pursuit of energy innovation, develop the next generation of leaders, and drive economic prosperity in Malawi. In both his early experiments and his late pursuits, the scarcity of materials or lack of funding did not hold Kamkwamba back nor hamper his ability to realize his leadership potential.

He had a vision of lighting his parents' house and irrigating the farmland. He turned the vision into action by building the windmill. His action and achievement inspired his village, his country and beyond. Despite all the challenges he faced, those challenges only ignited his flame of ingenuity and drive for action. Kamkwamba was not waiting to be empowered or asking anyone to let him build the windmill or establish the Innovation Center. Instead, he strived to create opportunities in life, and did not let anything or anyone stop him.

If I can use Kamkwamba's case to define what leadership is, I would say leadership starts with self-actualization. More importantly, however, it is the ability to inspire and influence others to turn vision into action!

According to Trainingindustry.com, the world spent about $370 billion in 2019 on various leadership development programs (Training Industry 2022). Yet, a good deal of leadership programs fail to create desired results in terms of motivating people to take leadership. "Too many training initiatives we come across rest on the assumption that one size fits all and that the same group of skills or style of leadership is appropriate regardless of strategy, organizational culture, or CEO mandate," says one McKinsey report.

Even to the basic question of "What exactly is leadership?" there is no simple answer. When Margaret Andrews, former Associate Dean for Management Programs at Harvard University, discussed leadership education in business school in a 2016 University World News article, she recounted the famous utterance by US Supreme Court Justice Potter Stewart in a 1964 case about obscenity (Andrews 2016). When asked whether he could define obscenity, Judge Stewart said he couldn't define the type of material that would be considered obscene, "but I know it when I see it."

"Leadership can be a bit like that," said Margaret Andrews. In other words, we simply do not know enough about what constitutes good leaders or how to develop transformational leadership. At the same time, we would know the presence or lack of a good leadership in many real-world scenarios.

I was very fortunate to have my education in two of the best institutions in the world, including a leadership class from world renowned leadership scholar Mike Useem from the Wharton School of Business, and academic leaders such as James Wei at MIT. I also attended countless leadership trainings and executive programs specifically designed for business leaders. I had a rewarding and successful career managing global businesses, product development, investments, and many other aspects of business.

Yet, I often struggled with clarity in terms of what leadership really means throughout my career.

I mentored many talented and driven individuals, especially in the last few years of my employment. The more people I talk to about leadership, the more I realized my struggle was not unique. Everyone struggles. Even the best leaders only appear naturally gifted because we don't see the time and effort they invested over the years. It takes a lot of effort to become effortless.

In 2017, when I got an assignment in China, I started writing a regular leadership blog on LinkedIn, partly to share my experience with others, but also to help myself develop my mental framework to think about leadership and decision-making. Over a quarter million aspiring leaders around the world now subscribe to and read my weekly leadership blog and share their perspectives and stories about leadership. My engagements with readers have truly enriched my perspective and understanding of leadership. Many asked me about writing a book.

As soon as I retired in March 2022, I made the commitment to write this book on leadership as my first project as a way to give back to my quarter million followers.

The biggest disconnect for leadership development in many organizations is organization-focused, rather than people-focused. On the one hand, everyone in today's business world is expected to be a leader. On the other hand, leadership development initiatives, often "standardized," rarely devote the resources and efforts necessary to connect individual leadership values with organizational objectives.

My own leadership survey indicates that only 39 percent of aspiring leaders were ever asked by their organizations why they wanted to be leaders. In addition, many leadership development programs tend to focus on leadership skills, rather than instilling courage and conviction necessary to be leaders.

When bestselling author Simon Sinek was explaining his 2009 book, *Start With Why* (Sinek 2011), here is what he said. "Every single person, every single organization on the planet knows what they do. [...] Some know how they do it [...] but very, very few people or organizations know why they do what they do."

Leadership needs to start with why! Why do you want to be a leader? Different people will have very different motivations. Without the why, we will just react to situations, rather than espousing intentional leadership and being purpose driven.

From an individual perspective, the process is often a life-long journey of conscious self-discovery, sometimes facilitated by certain events or epiphanies in life which change how you think about leadership. Only by going through such a personalized process can one truly develop the mental clarity to guide one's leadership actions. Aspiring leaders have to take ownership of their own leadership development by understanding and crystalizing one's leadership values and purpose.

Many organizations embrace in their mission and vision statements that their people come first. What does it mean when a company put its people first? Even if 'people first' is not explicitly part of the mission statement, every organization needs leadership. Leadership starts with people.

As implied by the words "Odyssey" and "Becoming," there is no straight line for the journey of self-discovery on your quest for leadership. It is a long wandering voyage before you can find your own inner voice.

The Odyssey of Self-Discovery includes stories and insights from thought leaders, interviews with many executives, as well as my own experiences of triumph and struggle as a global business executive. It speaks to early to mid-career aspiring leaders who are looking at making a leap in maximizing their leadership potential. The book can also be a useful guide for those who are embarking on a leadership journey for the first time. Business school students may find much of the content relevant. Although many examples and cases are business oriented, most of the concepts should apply equally to any organizations even public or non-profit. My goal is to help readers facing their own leadership challenges to have a structured framework to think about their leadership journey.

The first part of the book describes the foundation of leadership value, and how readers can develop self-awareness to explore their own inner voices and better connect their values with organizational objectives. Effectiveness of their leadership can be enhanced by knowing what truly inspires and motivates them, but also how they ultimately define success as a leader.

The second part of the book describes what makes great leaders, and how they create organization vision, make decisions, and foster environments which enable people to find the best way to achieve organizational objectives. Successful leaders, regardless of what levels they are in the organizations, clearly define and communicate a vision for the team. They are willing to take charge and do not shirk from making decisions to accomplish short-term objectives, but also always have the mental clarity on what the long-term impact they are trying to create.

The third part explores how some of the leadership frameworks outlined in the book can be applied in five different use cases, and some specific leadership development topics, including topics of interests for aspiring leaders or leaders in a new environment. In addition, I include a few specific topics about approaches for driving changes or leveraging projects for demonstrating leadership. With the increasingly global nature of leadership, I also touch upon the cultural context of leadership.

The book concludes with the summary of a leadership survey I conducted as part of the book, including a list of common mistakes and a practical guide for aspiring leaders who want to translate the concepts in this book into action.

Although the book is organized as described, it is not intended to be a textbook and you do not need to read the book in order. In fact, many of the chapters, especially those in Part III, can be read independently. With that said, I strongly recommend you read Part I first since it is foundational to your self-discovery journey.

I have included a brief key takeaway at the end of each chapter. In addition, I also proposed a leadership exercise at the end of each chapter for you to ponder. They are not a to-do list, rather some exercises to prompt you to reflect. Taking a pause at the end of each chapter before you rush to the next chapter will force you to think about how you can turn the learnings into leadership action.

On the journey of leadership growth, you will learn many lessons: how to know yourself better, how to lead effectively, and how to make decisions based on a vision aligned with your fundamental leadership values. I am hoping this book can create an inflection point of the journey of your leadership development. Reading this book, or any leadership books for that matter, won't make you a leader. For the recommendations to truly become meaningful, these learnings have to be internalized and translated into actions through personalized reflections and intentional practices.

PART I

WHAT IS
LEADERSHIP

CHAPTER 1

LEADERSHIP WON'T COME AND FIND YOU

The purposeful leader understands the important role their story contributes to the clarity and direction of their leadership.

—QUINN MCDOWELL

"As you leave here to start the next leg of your journey in life, there will be days where you will ask yourself, where is all this going? What is the purpose? What is my purpose?" These are some rhetorical questions asked of the MIT graduates by Apple CEO Tim Cook at his 2017 commencement address (Cook 2017). Those are the same questions Cook struggled with himself for many years.

Cook went on to explain that he thought he would have the answers when he went to college, or decided on a major, or found a good job. That wasn't enough. Then, he just needed a few promotions. That didn't work either. It was always just over the horizon, around the next corner. He kept pushing ahead to the next achievement; kept asking the same question. Nothing worked. He tried meditation, sought guidance in religion, read great philosophers and authors; none truly brought satisfaction to his searching.

The fifteen years of twists and turns continued until he joined Apple when Steve Jobs launched the "Think Different" campaign to revive the struggling Apple. Steve Jobs knew Apple could really change the world. Cook stated that until then, he had "never met a leader with such passion or encountered a company with such a clear and compelling purpose, to serve humanity." It was just that simple, serve humanity.

It was in that moment that Cook finally felt that something clicked. He finally felt a company that brought together challenging cutting-edge work with a higher purpose; aligned with a leader who believed that technology which didn't exist yet could reinvent tomorrow's world; aligned with himself, and his own deep need to serve something greater.

Cook's speech was powerful and profound. Yet the moments of reflection came to him in mid- to later-career after many years of searching for meaningful achievements and successes. Cook, in his 2019 Stanford University commencement speech (Cook 2019), poignantly repeated what Steve Jobs said fourteen years prior, "Your time is limited, so don't waste it living someone else's life." Cook went on to say, "If you got out of bed every morning and set your watch by what other people expect or demand, it will drive you crazy."

HOW WILL YOU MEASURE YOUR LIFE

Many of us have the same struggle throughout our careers to live in greater alignment with our true self. While it is a beautiful thing that something deep inside, or our true self, is pushing us to go after the life we want, it can be a lifelong journey of quest and exploration. However, having those epiphanies will no doubt strengthen the guiding principles of our leadership.

Similarly, Harvard Business School Professor Clayton Christensen, whose seminal book on disruptive innovation fundamentally transformed how business leaders think about innovation, asked a question in his new book *"How will you measure your life?"* while he was fighting cancer. (Christensen 2012).

Humans have been pondering the reason for our existence for thousands of years, a question people often go through an entire life without ever resolving or even getting closer to a satisfactory answer. Many might default to measuring their lives by the obvious things, such as the number of awards they won, the amount of money they made, or the number of places they traveled. But here is what Dr. Christensen said in a 2016 *Wall Street Journal* interview (Hagerty 2020).

"When I pass on and have my interview with God, he is not going to say, 'Oh my gosh, Clay Christensen, you were a famous professor at HBS. He's going to say [...] Can we just talk about the individual people you helped become better people? [...] Can we talk about what you did to help [your children] become wonderful people?'"

Dr. Christensen's advice is simple but profound. It transcends faith or religion.

"Don't worry about the level of individual prominence you have achieved; worry about the individuals you have helped become better people."

Christensen asked the following poignant questions.

"Are you striving so hard to find success that you're playing the world's game rather than fulfilling your core desires? Do you ponder the differences between success and significance? And in the end, how would you measure your life?"

Christensen's book was finished at a time when he had just overcome the same type of cancer that had taken his father's life. As he struggled with the disease, the question became more urgent and poignant. The book was about the meaning of life in general and is very personal. He struggled with the same question many have been asking themselves.

Similarly, many of us struggle with translating the abstract concept of leadership into decisions we regularly make in our professional or personal life. Our purpose in life will no doubt affect how we internalize leadership. Considering Christensen's questions not only forces us to reflect on the question but also the urgency of doing so.

Here is an excerpt of what I shared with my son David when he graduated from the University of Virginia in 2019.

Life is short. You probably feel like you have plenty of time ahead of you but life is short, really short. It feels like just yesterday that I was at where you are. Thirty-seven years passed in a flash and could only be cherished in memories. It's so seductive to tell ourselves that we'll go after what we want when we have more experience, more money, or more time, but the truth is, that will never happen. Those are just excuses as masks for our fear. It's only when we admit our fears and recognize how they are holding us back that we can begin moving forward. Otherwise, by the time we finally wake up, the opportunities passed by, and we are old. Cherish the youth and be adventurous. Find something you truly love and enjoy. Don't let the noise of other's opinion drown out your own inner voice. And most important, have the courage to follow your heart and intuition. Take chances while you have the opportunity.

When it comes to our value and purpose, how we are raised can have a significant impact, and in turn how we internalize leadership.

I grew up in a small village in northern China. I have very fond memories of my childhood and the dirt road, rugged and zigzag, leading to my hometown. Every time I took that small road when coming home, and hiking on the hill across the village, I always felt a strong sentiment about the land my ancestor chose about three hundred years ago. Looking at the countless valleys and mountains, it seems they are trying to tell me the ups and downs of its long history.

Unforgettable childhood memories are still fresh in my mind. I vividly remember the air and even the smell of my hometown, the crow of the rooster, the creak of the gate. The sky was always clear and blue, and the water in the little creek in front of the village was clear and clean. Every time I have the opportunity to return to my hometown, we always walk along the same path along that small creek. During summertime, we would see many Morningstar Lily flowers beautifully decorating the side of the mountain. Between the peace and quietness, occasional birds chirping does wonders for the mind. I also remember my mother would, under a small kerosene lamp, teach me and my brother how to count using match sticks, or do math with abacus. The priceless influence of those early lessons had on our future education set the foundation for our future pursuits.

My father had more than his fair share of hardships through the wars, setbacks during the famines in the early sixties, turmoil during the cultural revolution, and health issues later in life. Yet, my father was always respected and loved by people throughout his civil service career in various local government roles, and long after his retirement. He worked hard throughout his life, yet always cared about people. I reflect that was how he was taught by his parents.

One thing I always remembered was his generosity and willingness to help others. He was a pillar to the family and the broader community. People sought advice from him, seeking help from him even until his last days of life. After he was forced to retire early due to a stroke, the community work gave him purpose and drive. During his last stage of life, while he was fighting late-stage cancer, countless people would take turns visiting, helping to care for him and still seeking counsel from him.

My father was respected for his intellect, but he was more admired for his integrity, generosity, and goodwill with people. Now, he is no longer with me in his physical form, but his teachings will still guide me through my life. I never realized the value of those teachings until I grew up. Those deep-rooted values lead to belief in myself to live life with drive, purpose, and courage. In turn, those values directly or indirectly influence how I internalize leadership and how I lead.

Each individual has his or her individual value. Naturally, we do not expect that we all internalize our values and purposes the same way.

LEADERSHIP VALUE REFLECTION

My upbringing and early life experience propelled me to work twice as hard to push ahead with the next achievement or career move. All in all, I consider myself really fortunate to have the opportunity to do technology work, manage businesses, develop investments, and work with startups. At the same time, I had the opportunity to travel around the world to about thirty-five countries for various businesses.

While the personal achievement was fulfilling, I slowly realized that climbing the corporate ladder, while important, was not the only option to find purpose in what I do. During the last few years of my corporate career, I spent a significant part of my time in coaching and mentoring young generation leaders, in the hope that they could shorten their learning curves and expedite their leadership development experience. Even after retirement, I'm still getting emails and calls very often from aspiring leaders seeking career advice.

While the business world is a very competitive place, I fundamentally believe we achieve our success by helping others achieve their dreams. At the same time, we would also find the purpose and values for our life aligned with our leadership value.

From the leader's perspective, we should help employees craft their roles so that when they venture outside of their formal responsibilities, they are contributing in ways that are fulfilling to them and benefit the organization at the same time. When employees find fulfillment, they are willing to go beyond their formal roles, such as taking up special assignments, organizing campus recruiting events, or dedicating time and effort to volunteer campaigns. Those extra-curricular activities not only create opportunities for them to practice leadership in a low-risk environment, but also give them a sense of purpose aligned with their personal value.

For what is the value of our work and lives if it does not help others, help our communities, or make the world a better place?

The second lesson through my global business experience is that the world is getting smaller every day. We need to recognize we are sharing the planet with billions of people with varying cultural backgrounds. With all the commonalities and similarities, we are bound to have differences. It is natural to expect that each will seek to advance their own interest, but it is critical to have a constant awareness of our responsibilities in a larger, interlinked, and interdependent world. In the context of business, we need to respect people with different background and different opinions. In a larger sense, we all have to learn to respect the differences for us to coexist on this planet.

Whether we're consciously aware or not, we learn from our roots and the way we were raised. In turn, those values will influence our leadership value and drive our purpose. There is no one right answer about leadership value and purpose of life. There will never be one. Humanity has been searching for the answer for thousands of years in vain. Yet, you will have to search and answer for yourself, because your leadership value will be dependent on the answer. Having purpose and clarity will drive your leadership decision-making. Once you have the clarity, you will be able to change your path, if needed, by taking intentional small steps toward your ideal vision.

ALIGNMENT OF PERSONAL VALUES WITH ORGANIZATIONAL OBJECTIVES

From an organizational perspective, values help us determine appropriate standards of behavior. A solid set of organizational values can do a lot in setting the tone for a positive workplace culture that governs how organizations expect people to act. Values can help define an organization's personality and provide a framework for success while reinforcing company-wide ethics. When organizational core values align with personal values, employees are happier, more inspired and motivated since their contribution has a positive impact on both the business results and personal satisfaction. On the other hand, the exact opposite happens when they are misaligned.

Imagine you are on a call with one of your most important overseas customers and the customer is experiencing quality issues with your product. The issue is impacting their business and they want to make sure it does not happen again since you are the sole supplier, and their business is dependent on your product. Your boss assured the customer it was a onetime occurrence, even though you know full well the same issue has been occurring with other customers.

The false promise might save this customer for the short term. However, it is likely you will have an unhappy customer when the same issue occurs again. You will probably end up losing an important customer. More importantly, you lose the trust with the customer in the process. Furthermore, your boss is telling the team that similar behavior is expected and others will emulate the same behavior. An ethical leader would have owned up to the issue and work with the customer to resolve the issue in an earnest manner. The customer may still not be happy in the short-term, but they can make a plan for their business. You still have the trust of the customer and the opportunity to keep the relationship with them in the future. More importantly, an ethical leader sets the right behavior for the organization and team to follow by example.

Similarly, recent news reports suggest SpaceX fired a number of employees for publicly criticizing Elon Musk by sharing a letter calling Musk's behavior on social media "a frequent source of distraction and embarrassment" and asked SpaceX to condemn his actions (Bogage 2022).

Regardless of whether or not you agree with him, Elon Musk has created much drama in the public domain through his candid use of Twitter. It is natural to expect employees in those organizations would feel emboldened that they have the cultural permission to speak out publicly like this, since they were simply emulating his leadership behavior. If you are an organizational leader, I think this is a great example of how your actions shape the actions of those around you. Of course, the irony of the SpaceX story is Elon Musk, intentionally or unintentionally, created a culture he did not want his employees to follow.

While I was finishing up the book, Musk decided to acquire Twitter for $44 billion. It will be interesting to see how the acquisition will change the culture of Twitter and in turn his own companies including Tesla and SpaceX.

All too often, leaders say one thing and do another while at the same time asking their people to do as they say. These days, leadership by demand no longer works in most organizations. Modern employees want to see you in action, leading by examples. When your actions are not consistent with what you say, you will quickly lose the trust of your team as a leader.

Many organizations and leaders make the mistakes of assuming performance equals value and purpose. The alignment of organizational values with personal values is critical to have motivated and engaged employees. It is natural for business to focus on shareholder return, but leaders have to craft a set of values and actions that become a long-term commitment beyond shareholder value in order to engage and motivate employees, especially the younger and more idealistic generations. The recent Great Resignation is at least partially driven by the shift in expectations between personal values and organizational expectations in terms of working culture post–pandemic.

Swiss psychiatrist and writer C. G. Jung once said, "Until you make the unconscious conscious, it will direct your life and you will call it fate." Leadership doesn't just come and find you; you have to go out and intentionally get it. Otherwise, you will be living someone else's life. You will let someone else's value drive your leadership value.

IMPLICATION

Whether or not we are consciously aware or not, we learn from our roots and the way we were raised. In turn, those values will influence our leadership value and drive our leadership purpose. The more clarity we have about our own leadership value through self-reflection to understand why we want to be a leader, the more likely we will be able to make leadership decisions based on a consistent set of principles, rather than simply respond to the situations at the moment.

LEADERSHIP EXERCISE

Identify three reasons why you want to be a leader. Ask yourself how those reasons are aligned with your core values, and how those values are aligned with your organization's objectives.

CHAPTER 2

LEADERSHIP IS NOT ABOUT YOU

———

When you accept a leadership role, you take on extra responsibility for your actions towards others.

—KELLEY ARMSTRONG

Mao Zedong, the paramount leader of China, died on September 9, 1976, three weeks after I turned fifteen. I still remember exactly where I was at the time. People were standing around a radio in the only village store, all quietly listening and not sure how to react. The world seemed turned completely upside down even for someone who lived in a remote rural Chinese village. At least that's what I thought at the time.

A month later, the so-called Gang of Four including Mao's wife was arrested and soon afterwards, Deng Xiaoping, purged by Mao during the Cultural Revolution and rehabilitated as vice premier, had decided to tackle education as his first national priority while he was hatching his plan for the historic economic reform in China.

As a fifteen-year-old attending high school, I followed what was happening but barely appreciated the true significance of the events at the time which would eventually precipitate one of the most significant transformations in Chinese history and became a profound turning point in the life of millions in China.

Some of the changes happened dramatically overnight, while other things did not happen fast enough. During my two years of high school, which overlapped the tail end of the chaotic Cultural Revolution years, we barely had any normal class learnings until after Mao died, when there was a sense that the world seemed to be changing. Parents and teachers started encouraging us to study. However, I had only about two months before I finished high school in January 1977. Without much of a choice or option, I was soon sent away from home for mandatory re-education in a remote farm village. Attending college never once crossed my mind and was never something I could even have dreamed of.

Everything happened in a rush when the news came in the summer of 1977 that nationwide college entrance examinations would resume for the first time since 1965. An accumulation of ten plus years of high school graduates would compete, with much excitement and anxiety, for the limited spaces across the country for the opportunity to attend college.

Official figures showed that 5.7 million candidates signed up nationwide for the exam. Only 272,971 were admitted at an admission rate of 4.78 percent (Wu 2017). Most of the admitted were already in their 20s, or even their 30s. Considering the limited formal classes we had during high school, I did okay, but not good enough to be one of the lucky 272,971.

Disappointed but not discouraged, realizing for the first time in my life that college education could be a real possibility motivated me to dedicate the following several months to prepare for the exam again less than a year later. While continuing to work at the farm, preparation for the exam became the sole focus in my life. The long hours of hard work paid off next year when I was accepted by the Taiyuan University of Technology (Taiyuan Engineering Institute at the time) where the initial foundation for my chemical engineering career was set. I will never forget the smiles on my parents' faces when the letter of admission arrived at my home.

We all know that China has completely transformed itself since then, but I never could have imagined just how significantly it would impact my personal life in the coming years.

Unbeknown to me at the time, all my life journey was made possible by a personal decision made by Deng Xiaoping on August 13, 1977, in a meeting held at the Great Hall of the People in Beijing. Deng personally called the meeting with thirty-three senior educators, including university presidents and respected scientists (Li 2017). Deng's intent for the meeting was to ask for their input about how to resurrect higher education in China as a top national priority in order to revive China's then moribund economy after the disastrous prior decade. After some initial hesitation, several prominent educators brought forward concrete needs and concerns.

To his surprise, Deng learned during the meeting that a national conference was already held a week prior on August 4, coincidentally in a hotel less than two miles from where I eventually attended college. Attendees at the August 4 meeting had already developed and submitted a formal recommendation to the Chinese State Council to restart college admission the following fall in 1978. Fall admission was not only the norm, but also gave the bureaucrats and colleges sufficient time to prepare for the massive undertaking.

As the meeting went on, the consensus gradually changed. The attendees recognized that they were bestowed with an unprecedented opportunity to change the trajectory of China's education system.

"Don't waste another generation of talents." Deng challenged the officials in charge to expedite the process by departure from the norm. He adamantly demanded the officials to simplify the bureaucratic approval process for candidacy, and to revise the official recommendation to the state council.

Deng's personal intervention prompted the official announcement two months later of the resumption of college admission and the hectic preparation process to proceed with the unprecedented national college exam on December 10, 1977.

The decision allowed the first group of students to attend colleges in over a decade in March 1978, an unusual time to start a school year, but extraordinary circumstance calls for extraordinary measures.

I was not among the lucky 272,971 but had the chance to retake the college exam on July 20, 1978, and started college the same year on October 16, 1978. Many of the students from those two classes would eventually become key players in leading the transformation of China in the subsequent decades.

Some say it was a miracle the process happened that quickly, but it was, in fact a perfect example of leadership. Deng Xiaoping recognized science and education would be the foundation for driving the changes needed for China to transform its economy.

He did not ask the team to study what was possible in the situation. Instead, he created a vision for the nation and personally challenged the team to achieve the impossible for execution. His leadership not only started the transformation of China as a country, but also fundamentally changed the life of a quarter of the population on the planet.

To me, the meeting on August 13 was a pivotal moment for China.

Not all of us will ever be in a position to make such monumental decisions, but everyone in the business world or any other organizations today is expected to be a leader and called upon to stand up and take a leadership role, no matter the experience. The decisions we make during our lifetime can have significant implications on ourselves, people around us, and the business or beyond.

This means we need to train everyone around us to develop the critical thinking skills for making decisions and lead in order for them to grow into leaders.

People are often constrained by existing management processes or practices, rather than focusing on keeping the new generations of employees constantly challenged, motivated, inspired, and for them to perform at their best. In the case of China's college exam, when monumental changes in the country were taking place, Deng's leadership-philosophy for change superseded the management-philosophy of the bureaucratic status quo. Similarly, a dynamic business environment requires leaders not to act with yesterday's logic to deal with today's turbulence.

LEADERSHIP IS A RESPONSIBILITY

Leadership means different things to different people. It is always a struggle to personalize leadership and to translate leadership into decision-making and action.

Twenty years ago, when I was at Wharton attending the executive MBA program, I had a fantastic opportunity working with the Red Sox new owner John Henry and management team, including new CEO Larry Lucchino, on a class project about the business strategy development process. A small team of us, about six students, had the rare opportunity to see firsthand the decision-making process of the management team.

One of the unique experiences was attending the Red Sox spring training camp at Fort Myers, Florida and watching the spring training games with the team owners and top management in the owner's box. Sitting in the spacious owner's box with food and drinks, the owners and team executives were discussing business issues while casually watching the games on the field right down below.

One moment more ingrained in my head than anything else was the scene of decision-making by Mr. Henry at the time. It was a game between the old rivalry New York Yankees and Red Sox at the top of the third inning. One of the Red Sox prospects was pitching against the Yankees, and he gave up two hits in a row. John Henry, watching attentively while asking probing questions, made a decisive comment about this prospect, "he is done."

While the player continued pitching on the field, I kept thinking at the time that the young player, not aware of the decision already made, was still making his best effort in the hope of making the team, yet his fate as a Major League Baseball player was already sealed. Mr. Henry obviously knew what he was doing in terms of baseball decisions based on the fact that the Red Sox won the very first World Series the following year in 2004 after eighty-six years of frustrations for the team and the city of Boston.

As I reflect on that moment, I realized the decision was not unique by any means. Players get evaluated and rejected all the time. Likewise, venture capitalists turn down over 95 percent of applicants before they choose to invest. Ivy League schools reject over 90 percent of its applicants each year. All of us, especially in the corporate world, get evaluated and assessed on a regular basis. While those being rejected should find resilience and perseverance to move on, leaders, as the decision makers, should always be cognizant of the fact that their decisions, however necessary and rational from organizational perspective, have consequences on people's life, either positive or negative. Being a leader comes with awesome responsibility to the organization and the people involved.

You probably know that Stephen Curry is one of the most talented NBA basketball players who has led the Golden State Warriors with four NBA championships. What you may or may not appreciate is his willingness to take responsibility as a leader. After a recent conflict between two teammates boiled over and became national news, Curry promised they would figure it out, "That's what the job entails. Even if it doesn't, I've assumed that responsibility. Because everything does matter in terms of making sure everybody's experience is fun, is enjoyable, is memorable [...] I don't want to be too somber. But these, like, inflection points, these moments can make or break a team. And my job is not to let it break us at all." (Thompson 2022)

We often hear people lament their lack of authority, but the stories left us with only one possible conclusion. Authority comes only after a leader demonstrates willingness to take responsibility. This is not only true for top executives and leaders of nations, but also for anyone who aspires to be a leader.

Both Deng's action about China's college education and Mr. Henry's decision about the baseball prospect had significant consequences to their respective organizations. At the same time, those decisions also had direct or indirect implications on people's careers and lives. If you are aspiring to be a leader, you should realize leaders manifest responsible behavior through a willingness to take charge, not shirk from decisions or making excuses, especially during difficult times.

IMPLICATION

Leadership is first and foremost a responsibility, being responsible for the organizations, for decision-making, and for the people you are leading and owning the decisions you make. Leadership actions can have significant consequences on people's careers or even life trajectories.

LEADERSHIP EXERCISE

As an exercise of self-reflection, identify three defining moments in your life or career that either challenged or reenforced certain fundamental values you held, or something that invoked a strong sense of self-awareness. What did you learn from those moments and how have you applied those lessons in your leadership for making decisions?

CHAPTER 3

EXPLORING YOURSELF BEFORE EXPLORING THE WORLD

The most important conversations you'll ever have are the ones you'll have with yourself.

—DAVID GOGGINS

"I know exactly what we need to do." He very confidently told me in a taxi in Beijing, heading back to the hotel after a meeting with a major Chinese business partner.

It was a beautiful day in Beijing and the executive was in a very good mood. The meeting went well, and both parties were cautious but courteous. The person was an experienced executive with decades of global business experience, but I learned in the taxi that it was his first ever visit to China.

He went on to explain to me that he had worked in another Asian country on a similar business deal over a decade ago. He had apparently assumed the business environment and relationship would be exactly the same! It was a different country and about fifteen years apart. For those who have been doing business in China, nothing looks the same after fifteen years.

Right at that moment, I realized there would be tremendous challenges for us going forward. However, I was at a loss on what to say and what to tell him other than sharing some gentle nudges about the complexity of business environment in China. In addition, we might not have as much leverage as he thought in the partnership.

The false assumption led to an impasse and misaligned expectations, which dragged out for almost a year until a new executive assumed the leadership role for the project.

That experience had a profound influence on me, and I have reflected on that moment in my head many times since. On the one hand, I reflected on my own leadership and influence skills. What could I have done differently to influence the decisions? What could I have done to establish more trust and credibility to tell him that the approach likely is not going to work? On the other hand, I also reflected on the interplay between self-confidence and leadership, especially in the Western business world.

Many, in fact, intuitively assume self-confidence is a critical competence for being a leader. However, self-confidence needs to start with self-awareness, which is a much more important competence to have for being a leader. Self-awareness makes one self-confident, but self-confidence without self-awareness is just arrogance.

Tasha Eurich, an organizational psychologist, researcher, and New York Times bestselling author, cited a study in a Harvard Business Review article in 2018 that "even though most people believe they are self-aware, only 10–15 percent of the people we studied actually fit the criteria" (Eurich 2018).

People with high self-awareness understand who they are, where they are headed and what makes them motivated. By knowing their strengths and weakness, values, and aspirations, and how they affect actions and the actions of others, they are likely to be able to make better decisions and ultimately lead others.

INTEGRITY IS THE CORNERSTONE OF ALL SUCCESS

I once attended a lunch speech by Mr. Jeff Luhnow, then general manager of the Houston Astros in early July 2018, shortly after the team won their first ever World Series baseball championship in 2017. It was a much-needed win for the city of Houston shortly after the disastrous flood due to Hurricane Harvey that devastated a large part of the city. Mr. Luhnow explained how he led the transformational change of the Houston Astros from a historically poor professional baseball team in 2014 to its first ever world championship in a few short years. He shared some of the key decisions during the transformation: creating a vision, having the right people, leveraging digital technology, and being willing to take bold actions, all important components of what leadership is about.

A year later, whistleblowers revealed the Houston Astros had been using a sophisticated system to steal opposing team's signals to create an unfair advantage throughout the season, including the playoff.

According to a subsequent Major League Baseball investigation report, "virtually all of the Astros' players had some involvement or knowledge of the scheme." Even though Luhnow later denied any knowledge about the cheating scheme, the report stated Jeff Luhnow had at least some knowledge but might not have given it much attention (Hurley 2020). The scandal completely tarnished the reputation of the organization and all the leaders, including Luhnow, were eventually fired by the Astros. Remarkably, none of the 2017 Astros' players were disciplined by MLB, although "virtually all" of them were involved in this scheme in some way.

Ironically, I remember vividly Mr. Luhnow used the term "on the bleeding edge" to describe learning through making mistakes. He admitted during the speech that he had made mistakes, including the releasing of J. D. Martinez, who later became a star outfielder with the Boston Red Sox.

"The key is to accept responsibility and learn from the mistakes." Assuming the MLB report was accurate, it seems Mr. Luhnow failed to take his own advice in this case by taking responsibility for the scandal.

This also reminds me of another example in the 2003 Carlsberg Cup soccer game between Denmark and Iran played in Hong Kong when Iranian player Alireza Nikbakht mistook a whistle from the crowd as being the referee's half-time signal and picked the ball up with his hands in the penalty area.

The referee gave Denmark a penalty kick, but following consultation with national team coach Morten Olsen, Morten Wieghorst intentionally missed the penalty as a token of fair play. Denmark lost 1–0. Wieghorst received an Olympic Committee Fair Play Award (Tong 2022).

Ethics is knowing the difference between what you have a right to do and what is right to do. There are some defeats that are more victorious than winning.

Both the Astros and the Carlsberg stories tell the moral principles about leadership decision-making. Although we are inherently motivated by different things associated with our emotions, including ambition, impact, or affinity, it is always important to have clarity of purpose and values which inspire us at a more fundamental level. To have the clarity of the purpose of being a leader would not only provide a guiding principle of your decision-making, but also help define your leadership value. "Sports do not build character; they reveal character." This is a quote often attributed to legendary basketball coach John Wooden. Whether this means being honest, fair, compassionate, or moral, character speaks to a person's value.

One of the most important components of self-awareness is about your own leadership values and purpose. Our upbringings and life experiences create and shape our beliefs and values, but one often goes through soul searching before we get clarity of our purpose. In most cases, our personal leadership purpose might be different from the organization's purpose.

However, it is okay as long as we can identify the way our personal purpose benefits the organization and contributes to its success.

In turn, our beliefs and values guide us in choosing our goals, guiding us on how to lead and shaping our decisions. When we remain blind to the meaning we give to our life experience, we transact life instead of living it. When we lead in accordance with our values, we lead with our strength.

Business ethics is the guiding principle for every decision you make. What does this mean for leaders? Leaders have their own individual values, but more importantly leaders are responsible for defining the values and purpose for their organizations. Company values are the underlying philosophies that guide a business and its employees and influence the way a company interacts with partners, clients, and shareholders. Most large corporations have a set of core values that capture the essence of their business and culture. The ultimate value of values is not just shaping leadership behavior, but shaping the right leadership behavior. Whether leaders pay attention to company culture, culture will develop. Just like all people have personal values and unique personalities that inform their decisions and behavior, the business's values will influence how employees, customers, and other shareholders are treated. Of course, the way employees, customers, and other shareholders are treated has a huge impact on whether a business will ultimately succeed.

When an organization goes astray, it is inevitably a reflection of the integrity of leadership. Likewise, as individual leaders, you need to always have mental clarity and strong boundaries in terms of business ethics. Your integrity and credibility are your most important assets as a leader. They are powerful when developed, but devastating once you lose them.

KNOW YOUR STRENGTHS AND WEAKNESSES

We have all heard the fable of some hero entrepreneur in a suburban garage who stumbled upon the next big thing, thereby single-handedly revolutionizing their industry and becoming insanely rich in the process. But those fables often miss the twists and turns on the journey. In fact, Jeff Bezos went to Princeton University and his original plan was to study theoretical physics, he recalled in a 2018 Economic Club interview.

"I wanted to be a theoretical physicist. So I went to Princeton and I was a really good student. [...] I got A-pluses on almost everything." One day he stuck with a math problem. "I can't solve this partial differential equation. It's really really hard."

He went to his roommate Yashantha, who stared for a while and said cosine was the answer, followed by writing out three pages of detailed algebra. Bezos had one of those defining moments,"... that was an important moment for me because it was the very moment when I realized I was never going to be a great theoretical physicist. [...] I saw the writing on the wall, and I changed my major very quickly."

This is certainly a reflection of the high level of self-awareness by Bezos.

"We cannot be objective with ourselves. A leader is not allowed to label themselves a great leader." This is a comment shared by Martina Angelique Wagner, CEO of ArtesHumanis, on one of my LinkedIn leadership posts about self-awareness.

First of all, self-awareness includes the identification of one's strengths and leveraging those strengths. Very often, our strengths are developed and accumulated through experiences and setbacks. We often undervalue what we inherently do well because we tend to assume things that are easy for us will be easy for others. As a result, knowing one's strength is not always easy, but it is important to reflect on the context in which you thrive. Identify the elements where you flourish.

Are you better at starting something new or improving something existing? Do you thrive in a prescriptive environment with clearly defined tasks, or do you prefer ambiguity and having the latitude to figure it out on your own? Are you generally good at delegating to others or prefer more to be part of the action?

Second, leaders need to have a conscious reflection of their own weakness, which often manifests as unconscious biases. This is most challenging because solicitation of honest feedback on our biases and weakness, however transformational they could be, is not easy. When it comes to our own weakness, we tend to have blind spots. Willingness to look at ourselves through others' eyes helps us glean invaluable insight into how our emotion or communication style affects other people.

This is especially important in today's global economy, facing very diverse cultures and varied business environment. For example, in their famous 1998 book *Riding the Waves of Culture* (Trompenaars 1998), Fons Trompenaars and Charles Hampden-Turner shared a survey from around the world about what people thought were the main reasons for companies to have organizational structures. While many European country respondents thought it was for everyone to know how functions are allocated and coordinated, 30 percent of respondents from some Middle East countries thought the reasons for an organizational structure were to know who has authority over whom. A strength working in one culture may very quickly become a weakness if you are expected to behave in a more "authoritative" manner as a leader. Similarly, while providing frank and blunt feedback is expected and desirable in a country such as the Netherlands, the same behavior would be considered rude and impolite in some other countries.

If you are surrounded by others who share your perspectives, your career paths, and your outside interests, it's important to understand how your bias manifests with your teams and your leadership styles. Inclusive leaders need to maintain an objective and healthy perspective by tapping a wide range of different viewpoints. Informal networks are a powerful advantage for many who share the same perspectives, same interests, and same cultural background, which could potentially reenforce unconscious biases. Inclusive leaders need to be vigilant about not only how decisions are made but also who gets heard and who gets excluded from those discussions, especially in the increasingly virtual business world with people working in remote locations, including many on the other side of the world. We are human, and we all have natural biases. Very often, having an open mind, stepping back, and challenging the basic assumptions are warranted and necessary.

As our career progresses or the external business environment changes, knowing our strengths can offer us a better understanding of how to deal with our weaknesses and help us gain the confidence we need to address them. On the other hand, sometimes our strengths can become weaknesses. For example, experience can lead to a false sense of confidence about our performance, it can also make us overconfident about our level of self-knowledge.

Finally, I will point out that strengths and weaknesses are the common framework used in many organizations for performance evaluations. My experience is many leaders do not use the feedback process effectively due to lack of specificity of actionable recommendations on how to enhance their leadership by leveraging their strengths. People often walk away from the process with a negative feeling due to the one or two areas for improvements, instead of drawing specific lessons on how they could build on their strengths for development and growth. This is something aspiring leaders should consciously reflect on either when they are being given feedback or they are providing feedback to others.

HOW YOU ARE PERCEIVED BY OTHERS WILL AFFECT YOUR EFFECTIVENESS

Ms. Rose Hall, senior vice president and head of Innovation Americas at AXA XL, a subsidiary of AXA Group, shared with me an exercise called the "one word" game to better understand her own traits and how she was being perceived by those around her. She asked friends and colleagues individually what one word they felt best described her. After polling twenty or so people, none of whom knew the others' answers, Rose was astonished to hear that nine of the twenty responses were identical: "intense!"

According to Oxford Languages, the definition of intense is "extreme force, degree, or strength; having or showing strong feelings or opinions; extremely earnest or serious." It gave her quite a bit to reflect on how she was perceived by others. Even more shocking was when she looked up the synonyms of "intense," which include many words with strong negative connotations such as frightful, excruciating, and vicious. That in and of itself is intense to hear!

That experience helped her to reflect on her leadership. Today, her intensity hasn't changed because it's part of who she is. What has changed, however, is how she harnesses it and uses it. She has since learned how to balance her intensity and use it as her superpower in some situations and tuck it away in others. She could have looked upon "intense" as a negative, harsh thing she had to change about herself. Instead, she decided to develop it as one of her strengths. In fact, everyone can use their inherent traits as their own personal power, leveraging them to their advantage.

Knowing ourselves better is important, but knowing how we are being perceived by others is also an important part of self-awareness. Some might think I know who I am, and I do not care much about how others think about me. It is not wrong to think that we should figure out what is right and not care what other people think. However, in the context of leadership development and self-awareness, how you are being perceived by others can have impactful consequences regardless of whether the perception accurately reflects our true identities. The perception can and will affect one's effectiveness in the organization. People who know how others see them are more skilled at showing empathy and taking others' perspectives into their decision-making, or in Rose's case, leverage that awareness of intensity as her strength.

I joined ExxonMobil as an experienced hire in 2005 when I was forty-five years old. Although the business practice has changed somewhat today, it was fairly rare at the time for ExxonMobil to hire experienced people, especially at the management level. For employees directly recruited from college campus, there is a very structured process for their career planning and development. For people hired with years of experience, however, outside experience was less appreciated and valued. The perception people had would be that you are new to the organization, and many would be hesitant to assign important projects to you. As demonstrated in this example, it does not matter if you agree or disagree with the perception, it will have implications on your career unless you proactively manage your career and change those perceptions.

It is hard to know how you are being perceived and nobody is going to proactively tell you directly. In order for you to get honest feedback on how you are being perceived in the organization by others, one option is to identify mentors who have been in the organization long enough to share some insights. Rose's approach is a very effective one to get some insightful feedback. Another option is to create a culture of feedback by sharing helpful feedback with your colleagues to establish trust so they are more likely to share feedback and perceptions with you.

KNOWING THE CONTEXT OF YOUR WORK ENHANCES YOUR LEADERSHIP DEVELOPMENT

Another aspect of self-awareness is about seeing the big picture around your work and having an appreciation of what are the key issues and concerns of your stakeholders. It is important for everyone, but especially important for those who aspire to be leaders.

Some managers or engineers may think that all individuals and small teams need to know is their own piece of the project. The reality is open communication on a big picture perspective not only reduces the likelihood of miscommunication, conflict, and suboptimal performance within the team, but also increases motivation to get the work accomplished and commitment to the overall initiative. In addition, seeing the big picture allows team members to share insights and ideas and allows better integration and synthesis of different parts of a project toward the overall objective. From a personal development perspective, knowing the big picture also enhances the ability for team members to communicate with management or other team members of the significance of their project or results.

Many projects in today's business world we work on and manage are complicated. They combine multiple technologies and disciplines and occur in environments characterized by multiple organizations and units, often located in different locations or different parts of the world.

As humans, we have a very difficult time seeing things if we don't know what we're looking for. A leader with better awareness would see themselves as part of something far greater than the individual. Knowing the big picture objective would certainly enhance the chance of success, not only for the project but also for their individual career as well.

Before you deep dive into the specifics of the project, it is always advised to understand and appreciate the relationship between your project and the overall business objective. This is especially important for early career team members to ask probing questions to better understand the context of the project. If there are uncertainties about the project, you should know as well.

How do my projects fit in the company's strategic objective? How is the success of the project going to be measured and why? How are the working products or results going to be used to make overall business decisions?

IMPLICATION

Self-awareness is not about diagnosing and treating our fears of inadequacy, but how to discover what is truly important to us through self-reflection and feed-backs from people around us in order to leverage our strengths to maximize our potentials. The more we learn about ourselves, the more confident we would be as leaders and the more joys we would find in the missions we pursue. Having high self-awareness can help you objectively evaluate yourself, align your leadership behavior with your values, making leadership decisions based on a set of principles, rather than emotion driven. The more you can make decisions based on a consistent set of principles, the more likely you will be perceived and trusted as a leader.

LEADERSHIP EXERCISE

As an exercise, I encourage you to develop two different narratives to introduce yourself with and without mentioning your work experience. The exercise would help you identify what is truly important for you. The more you know yourself as a person, including your strengths and unique capabilities, the more likely you can be a confident leader. Identify two of your strengths that you could leverage to further enhance your leadership through specific relevant activities and then reach out to two potential coaches/mentors who can provide honest feedbacks.

CHAPTER 4

BEING RIGHT IS NOT ALWAYS SUFFICIENT

———

It is an illusion that once upon a time managers could make their direct reports do whatever was needed. Nobody has ever had enough authority—they never have and never will. Organizational life is too complicated for that.

—ALLAN R. COHEN

"I was very much matter of fact, I thought that my actions were going to speak for me but really, words sometimes speak louder than actions."

That is how Ricky Rossello, the former governor of Puerto Rico, described with me his reflection of his leadership journey when he became the governor in 2017. After training as a chemical engineer from MIT and receiving his PhD in biomedical engineering from the University of Michigan, Ricky gained experience in entrepreneurship and politics by founding an advocacy group for the statehood of Puerto

Rico and a biomedical research company working on drug development.

At the time Rossello took office, the Puerto Rican government debt crisis posed serious problems for the government. To achieve an amicable resolution with creditors, Rossello had developed a plan to make fiscal reforms and austerity measures.

Upon his election, he not only had a vision for reforming the government, but also a very specific and action-oriented plan for executing the vision. He articulated his vision about why he had to take actions. "A lot of reforms are not going to work. But if you just stay put in a time of change that requires change, you're going to fail just by inaction."

He mentioned during our conversation that he even developed a mathematical model "for reforming the friction, the sort of momentum moving forward, the time dependency, what things you know, add to it, what things subtract from it, and so forth." In other words, he was very much focusing on the specific facts and assumed logically how things should work.

During the interview, he reflected that although his plan and credibility "got me in the door" and "it's good for project management for getting results, but was not very effective for getting the hearts of people." He reminisced about where he could have done more to emotionally connect with his people to share his visions and actions with people before initiating further changes after some initial successes.

Similarly, my conversations with Dr. Matt Poepsel also provided some interesting perspective about the role of influence when he transitioned from being a marine to a civilian, and then a leadership coach. In the military environment, the intuition about leadership tends to be command-and-control, mostly focusing on getting the mission accomplished. As he entered the civilian world, his first job as a product leader did not have direct authority over engineers, sales professionals, or marketing professionals. He had to learn how to use indirect leadership or influence, which is much harder but critical for success.

In the business world and especially in the context of leadership, influence without authority mostly refers to an internal mechanism to get buy in, based on credibility and trust, from key stakeholders within your organizations.

Leading and influencing have somewhat different connotations in the context of leadership. However, no leaders can lead in a vacuum and every leader needs to have the skills to influence others in order to carry out his or her vision.

In the business world, influence without authority is increasingly defined as an important leadership quality in today's matrix organization. All of us have experienced situations where success hinges on the cooperation of several people in your organization over whom you have no formal authority. Learning to make effective arguments for influence without authority is important in every facet of business activities. Successes of those initiatives, especially during time of uncertainties and time of change, can define individual career as well as business success.

ARISTOTLE'S PERSUASION MODEL

Recognize the importance of influencing or persuading others is nothing new. In fact, Aristotle had thought about exactly the same question for persuasion twenty-four hundred years ago. Aristotle proposed the framework that arguments were more persuasive when applied in three distinct but inseparable dimensions in his treatise, *Rhetorica:*

- Logos: appealing to logic–coherence, structure, facts, statistics, research
- Ethos: appealing to credibility–reputation, trustworthiness, presence, confidence
- Pathos: appealing to emotion–humor, metaphor, framing, images, storytelling

People with technical backgrounds, certainly including myself, often intuitively focus on the facts, logic, and statistics when we try to exert influence or drive change. We tend to assume that organizations should always choose the "right decision" which is based on facts and data. It is our human nature to want to be right, and we feel validated and important when we are right. More often than not, we get frustrated when the answers are seemingly so obvious to us, yet it is hard for them to be accepted by others. It can become even more frustrating when things start moving only after someone else pitches the same idea.

Once you reflect on those experiences where you were not able to influence the actions or decision makings of others, you would recognize what was lacking was typically not your technical expertise or your logic, rather your credibility, or lack thereof, in the organization. It is especially true if you are a junior or new member on a team, or a perceived "outsider" for whatever reason.

Scott McEntyre, managing director of NOVI Labs, shared his thoughts with me when we were discussing influencing vs. leading. "I was at Noble Energy in technical roles for 15–20 years before the current role, and I was really focused on being right and getting the right answer. When I started to switch to being a leader, I realized that it wasn't enough to be right. You got to build consensus. You have to get people to believe that you're right. [...] that's what I have noticed; the need to switch from being right to delivering the right answer through a teamwork approach is what has to happen."

Even building consensus will require the effort to establish trust and credibility with the team. Otherwise, it is likely the team will be dealing with conflicts rather than an aligned vision to move forward.

What does it take to establish credibility in an organization? Credibility is mostly based on two components: expertise and trust. Although expertise is the foundation for credibility, it is only necessary, not sufficient. Without trust, expertise is simply not going to be accepted by others or the organization. Trust is the enabler of any relations.

There is no universal roadmap on how to establish trust, but I will highlight two aspects: cultural difference and authenticity. There are significant differences in inherent trust level across different cultures. People in some cultures trust unless you prove otherwise, others do not trust unless you can demonstrate you are trustworthy. In a global business environment, a prudent approach is to be authentic and have transparent conversations to avoid misunderstanding or misplaced expectations.

The third component of Aristotle's persuasion framework is about emotion. While creating emotional connection is likely the key driver for influencers in the virtual world of social media, it is generally not how it works in the business world. In order to have emotional connection with those you want to influence, you have to take the time and effort to understand their priorities and concerns. The more you can understand their emotional needs, the more likely you can frame your message for emotional connection. It is not a manipulation but instead a way to have conscious communication in a way that will resonate with them.

I should emphasize that part of appealing to emotion also includes the ability to listen to the other side. It is through those emotional connections that both sides can create clarity, gain insights, and unearth the real truth. This is a skill which does not always come naturally for people with a technical background or people working in a different culture. One has to be intentional in developing those skills in order to excel.

It might be counterintuitive, but business leaders could potentially benefit from some of the skills politicians use for campaigning or governing, especially with increasing focus on environmental, social, and governance (ESG) in the business environment and the need to connect with both employees and the broad society.

Former vice president of ExxonMobil Chemical Technology Will Cirioli shared his perspective at a University of Florida interview, "A lot of times I think when you come from an engineering background, you feel like if you're right, then everybody else will just understand that and superior logic will prevail. So I think you have to learn a lot of influencing skills along the way. And you need to look at things from a different perspective. And as you progress as a leader you tend to do more through others. And so the key is to understanding things from a perspective of others. And that takes a lot of active listening" (UF Herbert Wertheim College of Engineering 2012).

At a macro level, digital technology and information transparency will continue to create more optionality and flexibility for the future of work, and as a result drive more of the younger generations away from the command-and-control type of environment. They want individuality and flexibility, but also want to be connected and inspired. The balance of power is shifting to those who can organize and persuade to create wins in organizations. The future of leadership will increasingly be about the ability to influence and persuade. Leaders must ensure people feel connected to the company's purpose and vision and also to each other.

Aristotle's ethos, pathos, and logos provide a clear and easy-to-apply framework for developing influence in an organization. With practice and reflection, we can all learn and grow. "We are what we repeatedly do. Excellence is not an act, but a habit." Aristotle said it well.

TWO CIRCLE THEORY OF LEADERSHIP

If you want to exert influence in the workplace, you have to first intentionally identify your sphere of influence in order to make an impact on the business as well as your career. I want to share with you a simple mental framework I call "two circle theory of leadership". I have shared this with many early career employees over the years with good success.

Regardless of where you are in life and what you do for a living, we all have a job with a scope of responsibilities. With each job, there comes a job description, either written or more likely implicit. I call that scope the small circle. On the other hand, you most likely know that many things are completely outside of the scope of your job, defined by the space outside of the big circle. In an ideal world, the boundary would be clearly defined, and the two circles would be the same. In the real-world, however, those two circles do not completely align and there is always a gap between the two circles. When the job is well defined, the gap tends to be small. When the job is not as well defined, the gap can be very big. Regardless of the situation, how you handle the in-between space can define your success or failure in your career.

One can certainly focus on the small circle and do everything well within your defined boundary. Performing well in the small circle will help you establish credibility in the organization. However, simply focusing on doing your assigned job well in the small circle is very unlikely to make you a leader. On the other hand, you may not have the permission to venture outside of the big circle.

If you want to excel and be a leader, you have to be proactive and demonstrate your leadership in defining, leading, driving the activities between the two circles. The mistake early career employees often make is that they are afraid of taking initiative outside of their small circle and instead wait for instruction or ask for permission even when they have the capacity and capability to perform the tasks in in-between space. The right approach often requires employees to proactively engage their managers or simply take the initiative to perform the tasks.

The space between the small circle and big circle is also where leaders have the most flexibility to decide what they want to prioritize. For example, more and more people are seeking ways to exert meaningful influence on some of the society's biggest challenges such as the environment, inequality, and poverty. Employees who use the middle space to work toward such goals, especially when encouraged by organizations with a genuine sense of purpose, can boost a sense of empowerment and feel they are able to make a difference.

There are ways to demonstrate leadership in any situation, but the in-between space is the best place to do so by forcing yourself to stretch your capability, learn new skills, establish your credibility, and expand your sphere of influence.

In summary, if you want to lead your teams to thrive in the increasing complex world where power has shifted increasingly from hierarchies to networks, you have to shift your leadership mindset and skill set. Ability to influence without authority is a fundamental leadership skill in the workplace or the wider world.

IMPLICATION

For aspiring leaders who are seeking ways to exert meaningful influence in the workplace or the wider society, they have to shift their leadership mindset and skill set. While the traditional approach to leadership development tends to focus on moving up the management ladders, the current business environment requires aspiring leaders to be intentional about where and how to influence others.

LEADERSHIP EXERCISE

Define the scope of your responsibilities by using the two-circle framework. Identify two areas you can exert influence on between the two circles and develop a strategy of influence by using Aristotle's framework. Write out the specific approaches for each of the three aspects of persuasion.

CHAPTER 5

SUCCESSES COME IN ALL SHAPES AND SIZES

———

Success is stumbling from failure to failure with no loss of enthusiasm.

—*WINSTON CHURCHILL*

Matthew Emmons started out as a successful junior rifle shooter and won several world shooting championships, earning the world record for the fifty-meter rifle event. In his Olympic debut at the 2004 Athens games, he won the gold medal in prone position even though he had to use a borrowed rifle since his own precisely tuned rifle had been severely sabotaged before the games. Two days later in the three-position competition, however, he was less fortunate. He was leading until the very last shot when he misfired at another competitor's target. He not only lost the gold, but he also ended in eighth place (NBC Sports 2022).

Fortunately, or unfortunately for Emmons, that was not the end of the story.

At the 2008 Beijing Olympics, he won a silver medal in the prone competition. In the three-position event, Emmons again showed his excellent skills with a seemingly unsurmountable 3.3 points lead before the final shot. He only needed a 6.7 out of 10.9. Yet again, his finger "twitched" and prematurely hit the trigger. He scored 4.4. He again not only lost the gold but dropped to fourth place.

During an interview after the game, he was quoted as saying, "Life is too short to dwell upon the negative. There is nothing I can change about the past. I can only move forward."

Moving forward, he did.

He overcame thyroid cancer in August 2010, made the 2012 Olympic team and earned a bronze in the three-position event.

Some will always remember Emmons as the one who lost two gold medals, but he reminded himself that he was the one who "won an Olympic medal of every color!"

Successes are cause for celebration, but failures are typically not shared or talked about. Chances are, if you had not pursued the career, competition, or relationship, you would not have experienced the failures. If he chose not to compete in the Olympics, Emmons would have been remembered as the world shooting champion and world record holder for the fifty-meter rifle event. But he wouldn't have had the Olympic experiences either. Learn to see failures, along with the successes, as proof that you're brave enough to take on risks and to participate in the wide realm of experiences available on this planet. Feel empowered by what you have accomplished.

VINCENT VAN GOGH VS. PABLO RUIZ PICASSO

In a completely different world, both Vincent van Gogh and Pablo Ruiz Picasso are among two of the most influential figures in Western art history regardless of what standards you use. Yet their successes went through completely different trajectories.

I visited the *Picasso: Birth of a Genius* exhibition in Beijing in 2019. Pablo Ruiz Picasso (1881–1973) is probably the most important figure in twentieth century art. The exhibition retraced the journey of an extraordinary man whose long art career spanned between the classical and modern worlds. The exhibition illustrated how the young prodigy wowed everyone with his creative *Science and Charity* at a young age of sixteen by winning national acclaim at Madrid's Fine Arts Exhibition.

However, his focus on classical artistic expression was a very short-lived stint studying at the Academy of Fine Arts in Madrid. He subsequently not only succeeded in assimilating the lessons of ancient art and absorbing the newest expressions of his contemporaries, but also managed to develop new approaches, which fundamentally changed the trajectory of the development of modern arts. Picasso was an avid innovator and much of what characterized his work was his own, entirely original style. Picasso was at the forefront of developing the new artistic style of cubism between 1907 and 1908, a form which he refined continuously, but which remained prominent in his work throughout his life.

With a career that spanned almost eight decades and included success in painting, sculpting, ceramics, poetry, stage design, and writing, his tendency to experiment with his craft is unsurprising. However, the extent to which his style changed in each discipline—particularly in painting—is unlike that of any other artist. What's truly remarkable is that he never stopped reinventing himself throughout his life.

Picasso never stopped exploring and experimenting. Here is how he explained his philosophy of success. "Success is dangerous. One begins to copy oneself and to copy oneself is more dangerous than to copy others. It leads to sterility."

While creating or developing a unique style could be the ultimate success in the art world, Picasso looked at artistic styles very differently. "At the root of it, I am perhaps a painter without style. Style is often something that locks the painter into the same vision, the same technique, the same formula for years and years, sometimes for a whole life [...] I myself stir too much, move too much. You see me here, and yet I have already changed, I am already somewhere else. I am never fixed, and that's why I have no style."

In today's fast-moving world, there's a lot for us to learn from Picasso about what success means. We all could take his inspiration and be willing to try new ideas and adapt as technology changes the way we interact with the world. Keeping pace in a turbo-charged world means we need to make sure we don't dwell on short-term successes. Instead, we need to not only continue to learn but also to ignore the rules of the games, and sometimes go against the stream.

As a stark contrast, Vincent van Gogh had a very different life. My family visited the *Atlanta van Gogh Immersive Experience* on Labor Day in 2021. The exhibition was quite an awe-inspiring adventure to explore his work enabled by modern digital technology. The paintings come to life in an unimaginable way, leaving one in awe and wonder. More importantly, however, I learned more details about the journey of Vincent van Gogh.

In part of the exhibition, you have a chance to walk into the Starry Night Over the Rhône River as van Gogh had imagined, to see the vase in a dozen different flower arrangements that van Gogh must have experimented with, to stand in his Arles bedroom as how van Gogh had visualized in different settings, or to watch the sunflower fields as van Gogh experienced them. In addition, you see the 3-D recreation of his *Courtesan* as how van Gogh might have imagined the Japanese ukiyo-e (after Japanese Painter Kaisei Eisen). Finally, you learn the details of the discovery in 2020 by a French researcher of the actual tree roots that one of van Gogh's final paintings, *Tree Roots*, was based on two days before he died by a self-inflicted gunshot on July 29, 1890.

The exhibition illustrated not only van Gogh's life but also the places that inspired some of his most iconic paintings, including *Cafe Terrace at Night* and *Starry Night*, as well as experience how he painted some of the most iconic paintings including the *Sunflowers* and the *Vase with Flowers*.

Vincent van Gogh is one of the most influential artists of all time, yet he struggled in obscurity during his whole life and was never famous as a painter during his lifetime. He sold only one painting while he was alive, *The Red Vineyard*, which went for 400 francs seven months before his death. Before he became an artist, Vincent van Gogh also chased many vocations in vain in his youth, first as an art dealer in London, then briefly as a schoolteacher in England before working at a bookstore back in the Netherlands. He pursued a career in Christian ministry without success. A common theme in van Gogh's life persisted—failure after failure, disappointment after disappointment.

Vincent van Gogh, as an artist, never knew during his lifetime of the fame and fortune that would result from his greatness in art. On the other hand, the fact that he was not doing commission work might have allowed him the freedom to explore and experiment for the eventual success.

While we admire the enduring legacy van Gogh left behind for us to enjoy one hundred thirty years later and likely generations to come, his life story also makes me wonder what career success really means. For some, failure doesn't mean you are a failure, it just means you haven't succeeded yet. For others, it is not what you achieve, but it is what you overcome that will define your career. Though he did not know during his lifetime, Vincent van Gogh was both, yet much, much more. The tragedy is that the world did not appreciate his greatness in art before his suicide after years of depression and poverty. Life often unfolds in mysterious and miraculous ways. We just need to embrace it as it comes along.

While Picasso had the freedom to explore and experiment throughout his life at least partly due to his fame and success. Vincent van Gogh found his freedom at least partly due to the struggles he had throughout his life.

YOUR SUCCESS CAN ONLY BE DEFINED BY YOURSELF

Leadership means different things to different people. Many view it as a necessary skill set to enable their career success. However, the van Gogh and Picasso stories also illustrate the vast difference in term of career success. As a result, the required leadership qualities are also very different.

Fundamentally, one needs to know why you are interested in leadership. Do you want to be a leader as an enabler for you to pursue what you want to pursue, or do you just want to be a leader because that is the standard path to career success? Do you want to be a leader so that you can have more impact on the organization's mission? Would being a leader make you happy and enjoy life more?

At some point in our lives, we find out why we are here. I believe that we all have a function, a purpose, a job to do in this life. Some have developed their purpose and value early through their upbringing, others have to struggle through a turbulent journey.

My conversations with Phil Dearing, co-founder of Second Day, amplify this point. Second Day was founded to bridge the talent gap in social impact. Phil shared with me how the organization was aligned with his life's purpose.

Phil grew up as a Christian with the Methodist Church in Missouri. In high school, he started leading activities such as helping repair housing after storm damage or help Native Americans to improve their housing and living conditions. The early involvement made him see and experience the power and motivation of people all working toward the greater good, which was inspirational.

At the same time, he realized it did not matter how many nails he could hammer in one day. "If I could give a speech and motivate 200 other people to work five or 10 percent harder, that would get far more done than I could ever do like myself and so that really internalized with me in high school, and it continued throughout my life in college." He started a community service group that helped motivate other Georgetown University students make service more accepting and more accessible during college. However, he felt isolated and lost trying to figure out what career options existed and how to try to navigate launching a career in social good.

Two years ago, he, working with co-founders, started Second Day, an organization dedicated to bridging the talent gap in social impact. The name Second Day refers to the following quote from Mark Twain, "The two most important days in your life are the day you are born and the day you find out why." There is an increased calling from younger generations to be involved with social impact, but it is always a challenge to find what career opportunities exist that have social impact. The talent gap refers to the pattern of 60 percent of millennials reporting that mission is an important part of their career, but only 20 percent entering the industry in any capacity. They wanted to identify the root causes behind the gap and narrow it by unlocking more high-potential talent who dedicate their careers to untangling some of society's most complex challenges.

Success can be defined by the impact one creates, but can also be self-discovery.

For those who grew up thirty years ago, *The Wonder Years* was one of the twenty best TV shows in the late 1980s. It depicted the story of the transition from child to adult during the turbulent social times of the late sixties. It was listed by *Rolling Stone* in 2016 as one of the 100 Greatest TV Shows of All Time (Sheffield 2016). Danica McKellar, who played Winnie Cooper, was one of the main characters for the show and obviously had great success. However, she eventually left her acting career and pursued a mathematics career. She later wrote eleven non-fiction books, all dealing with mathematics. During a recent interview (Garvey 2022), she explained her decision. When she attended UCLA, everywhere she went, she could not get away from people who would shout "hey Winnie." She went on and discussed how she needed to figure out what her value was. "I needed to find out how I was valuable outside of Winnie Cooper, and math was challenging and I did well at it. And I love this feeling that my value, the important stuff had nothing to do with how I looked or television."

It is likely you have introduced yourself on a daily basis without having given much thought to its importance. It became more interesting or agonizing after I retired. If you have tried the leadership exercise in Chapter 3 by introducing yourself without mentioning your job or title, it would force you to think about who you really are and what you value the most about yourself. Even if you are introducing yourself in a professional setting, how you introduce yourself can send a very different signal to the other party, intentionally or unintentionally, by focusing on your expertise, your responsibility, or your seniority and title.

- "I am part of the product team at Company X."
- "I am responsible for the product design of business line Y."
- "I am the Senior Director of Product Design at Company X."

As a very different example of self-discovery, I interviewed Dr. Clotilde Bouaoud for this book, a scientist by training with a PhD in Physical Chemistry and experiences in the corporate world. She found that "science does not bring me purpose." She subsequently tried pole dancing, fitness, circus, and aerial sports to search for her identity and purpose until finally she jumped into entrepreneurship and followed her newfound purpose as a certified high performance coach in 2021 to help international entrepreneurs and leaders find the keys to sustainable high performance professionally and personally, so they can have the contribution they desire in the world while enjoying the best quality of life possible. In a recent video she posted on LinkedIn, she suggested that every single day, "I believe everybody should ask themselves how can I enjoy myself more? How can I make today exciting work?" Her advice to others was to follow what drives you and listen to your intuition, stay in your lane no matter what others think, fight for your own happiness in all areas.

Life is sometime serendipitous. You do not always get what you want in life, you get what you get. However, you have to know what you want, what is important to you, and what success means to you as a leader. Only then can you chart your own path, make purposeful decisions, and make your own choices on what to hold on and what to let go with grace as a leader. The beauty of leadership lies in the fact that a person does not need to have any formal titles or place on the organization charts. People follow leaders because of their values, vision, purpose, and inspiration.

IMPLICATION

You should not let society define what success means for you. The worst thing in the world is to spend your life pursuing goals laid out by others. You do not always get what you want in life or career. However, you have to know what you want, what is important to you, and what success means to you as a leader. Only then can you make purposeful decisions as a leader.

LEADERSHIP EXERCISE

As an exercise, write out what success means to you in the short-term and long-term and reflect on how you would measure the success. Ask yourself why you made the choices you did. Is the definition of success you choose a journey or destination?

PART II

WHAT GREAT LEADERS DO

CHAPTER 6

CLARITY OF VISION HELPS PRIORITIZE

The greatest danger for most of us is not that our aim is too high and we miss it, but that it is too low and we reach it.

—*MICHELANGELO*

Four years after the Sputnik moment and a month after Soviet Cosmonaut Yuri Gagarin became the first human in space, President John F. Kennedy announced on May 25, 1961, before a special joint session of Congress the dramatic and ambitious goal of sending an American safely to the Moon before the end of the decade. It was a monumental commitment for the United States. A year later, President Kennedy delivered his more widely cited speech before a crowd of about 40,000 people at Rice University on September 12, 1962.

We choose to go to the Moon in this decade and do the other things ... not because they are easy, but because they are hard; because that goal will serve to organize and measure the best of our energies and skills, because that challenge is one that we are willing to accept, one we are unwilling to postpone, and one we intend to win, and the others, too.

Kennedy used for his speech to inspire the nation, "a characterization of space as a beckoning frontier; an articulation of time that locates the endeavor within a historical moment of urgency and plausibility," according to John W. Jordan, professor of communication at the University of Wisconsin–Milwaukee (Jordan 2003).

Kennedy defined a vision, set a goal which is specific, time bound, measurable. The goal was set not because scientists at the time thought it was feasible, but because the country needed to "catch up or overtake" the Soviet Union in the space race.

Likewise, companies and organizations often define their vision and mission statements. A mission statement defines the company's business, its objectives, and its approach to reach those objectives. A vision statement describes the desired future position of the company.

Those statements must include both a vision to inspire the organization, but also the specific goals so the organization can measure progress and achieve its objectives. When organizations set a lofty vision without specific, measurable and time bound goals, it is very hard for the organization to translate that vision into actions and align the organization. On the other hand, simply setting goals and objectives, such as financial targets, without the vision to inspire, is not sufficient to motivate the organization.

As a contrast, here is how former Secretary of Defense Dr. Robert Gates explained his take on the Afghanistan war at an Asia Society dinner event I attended on October 13, 2021. The event was to honor Dr. Gates, one of the greatest American civil servants, for his service but coincided with the recent collapse of the US-assisted institutions in Afghanistan in the wake of the US withdrawal. During his long and distinguished career, he managed to avoid partisan squabbles while working in the administrations of eight different presidents, including serving as the secretary of defense for both President George W. Bush and President Barack Obama.

> *We built the Afghanistan military based on the mode of US military and American supply chain, rather than a military which would be self-sustainable after US pullout. While the Afghanistan population needed wells for clean water and health care facilities, we built schools without knowing if there would be teachers.*

He shared some of his perspective about the mistakes the US made and lessons we learned in the Afghanistan conflict, including the failure to look at the war from the Afghan perspective and to collaborate with the Afghan society. In other words, the United States created a vision for the future of Afghanistan, but the vision never really resonated with the Afghan people. Although this is just his personal perspective, it is certainly a perspective that we should reflect as a nation.

The dramatic fall of Kabul, the rapid collapse of two decades of a US-led Western campaign to remake the country, was shocking to many Americans but hardly surprising. Likewise, having a clearly defined vision with the buy-in of the organization is equally important for businesses or any organizations.

During times of change and uncertainty, organizations often need to find ways to rally around purpose or aspirations. Governments are not the only institutions that must define their vision in times of uncertainty. Business leaders, too, must inspire their organizations with a common purpose.

In a letter from Google CEO Sundar Pichai to employees in early 2022, he pointed out the need to have sharper focus and more hunger with the headwinds that were affecting the rest of the economy. He described the situation in three words, "scarcity breeds clarity." Those three simple words effectively articulated the needed urgency for change and focus (Zetlin 2022).

Volkswagen, as one of the largest automobile companies in the world, has been facing many challenges in the last few years, in large part due to the diesel engine scandal when VW misled regulators and customers by installing software to manipulate emission tests. In addition, increased market competition from electric cars vs. its traditional platforms using internal combustion engines is also forcing VW to reassess its overall strategy.

Similar to most other automobile manufacturers, getting into the electric car business while trying to deliver for the core business has not been easy. VW announced last year that half of its sales are expected to be from electric vehicles by 2030 and almost 100 percent of its new vehicles in major markets should be zero emission vehicles by 2040. At the same time, the valuation of Elon Musk's Tesla has surpassed the next five largest car companies combined, VW being among them.

In order to spur innovation and galvanize his organization, Herbert Diess, CEO of VW, invited its main competitor, Tesla CEO Elon Musk, to call in to an internal conference with 200 VW top executives (Dow 2017). The purpose of the conference reportedly was to get VW executives on board with the massive changes VW would need to make to confront the changing auto industry by "making faster decisions, less bureaucracy, more responsibility." Herbert Diess tweeted after the meeting, "with a new mindset and a revolution in our headquarter Wolfsburg, we can succeed the new competition. [...] Big responsibility at a crucial point for our company."

Many in the traditional industries that are being disrupted can probably resonate with those statements in the increasingly fast pace of changes of today's business world due to global competition, uncertainties in the future of work, changing technology, but especially increasing societal call for action for businesses on environmental, social and governance (ESG).

At a more fundamental business level, this is also intertwined with the debate between business strategy solely focused on shareholder value vs. stakeholder value. The idea that the sole purpose of a firm is to make money for its shareholders got going in a major way with an article by Milton Friedman, the winner of the Nobel Prize in Economics in 1976. The concept was further cemented in place by the policy statement from Business Roundtable CEOs in 1997 on "maximizing value for shareholders as the sole purpose of a corporation." I remember my economics professor at Wharton explained to the class how focusing on shareholder value was the best way to ensure the interests of other stakeholders would be covered.

Businesses are not designed to solve societal problems. However, focus on environmental, social, and governance considerations is increasingly pushing those non-financial factors into the analysis process companies use to identify material risks and growth opportunities while being aligned with societal objectives. Companies are increasingly recognizing the need to define and communicate clearly their ESG objectives, not just for analysts and regulatory purposes, but also for attracting, motivating, and retaining the next generation of talent.

Employees, especially the new generations of employees, need more. Born in the digital age, the new generations of employees are more socially aware and environmentally responsible. According to The Global Risks Report 2020 by the World Economic Forum, the younger generations show more concern about environmental issues and ranking them as the top risks in both the short and long-term (World Economic Forum 2020). As a result, members of the millennials and Gen Z generations are more likely to see themselves as ESG stakeholders. Consequently, they need to be challenged by an organization's mission and inspired by a purpose which is more aligned with their individual values.

Some might think that setting the vision and mission of an organization are the sole responsibility for top management and aspiring leaders have little chance to influence those decisions. In reality, it is equally important for any organizations or teams you lead to have a clearly articulated purpose, regardless of the size of the organization. If you are leading a team within a large organization, you need to translate the overarching vision of the organization into something specific your team can resonate and connect with.

I had a recent conversation with David Olivencia. Born and raised outside of Chicago, he always had a strong affinity with the Hispanic community since his family came from Puerto Rico. He organized a group of like-minded, passionate people and together founded an angel investing group to grow Hispanic and Latino ventures and support diverse founders and startups who are pushing innovation within their respective industries. The group recognized that currently Hispanics only made up 2.3 percent of the US angel investors, while the Hispanic population is about 18.5 percent of the total population. They embarked on a vision to correct those statistics to support the community. In particular, they felt strongly that there were significant investment opportunities, since the community is currently so underserved. The fund has quickly grown from an idea to about one hundred members and a portfolio of fifteen companies with a target to grow to 175 members in three years.

Another example is based on my personal experiences. With 1.4 billion people in China, it is an important market for many businesses. One of the challenges for local Chinese employees in multinational companies is the limited career growth opportunities when decision-making power tends to stay at the headquarters outside of China, especially for companies without a large local presence.

From 2017 to 2020, I led the development of investment opportunities in China for ExxonMobil. While the overall business objective was to grow business in China, many of the local team members were much more excited at the prospect that the investment would naturally expand the business footprint and create more career growth opportunities for local employees as the business grows. The two objectives are not inconsistent, but the latter resonated and connected with the employees at a more personal level. As a result, we would emphasize the career opportunities when we communicated about the project with employees and the team. Whenever possible, you want to create or define an identity for your team or organization which is aligned with the overall vision but is also translated to a level of specificity which the people involved can feel more connected to.

Most organizations have a strategic planning process, and it has its role in deciding on the strategic direction for the organization. However, in an increasingly uncertain time and fast-changing environment, leaders need to think about vision, not just strategic planning. A vision says something that clarifies the direction in which an organization needs to move. Clarity of direction is crucial in order to inspire organization and people through changes by being adaptive, agile and ready to do what it takes to survive and thrive in fast-changing market circumstances.

What works for organizations works for individuals as well. Having a clear vision of what really matters to you in life is also a prerequisite for success on your leadership journey.

BBC recently reported a study by Dr. Emily Balcetis, a behavioral scientist at New York University, who asked two groups to walk quickly to a finish line while wearing ankle weights (Taan 2021). The first group was the baseline group. They were instructed to walk as they normally would. The second group was trained to keep their eyes solely focused on the finish line. Before the task, both groups were asked to estimate the distance to the finishing line. The second group saw the finish line 30 percent closer than the baseline group. After the task, the study showed that the pace for the second group also increased by 23 percent. Nothing changed about the exercise itself, but the visual focus changed their mindset and mental focus.

The implication of the study is that it is possible to change the way that we see the world by having a clear vision that we can consciously focus on.

In summary, a clear vision provides not only a sense of purpose, but also a laser focused view of the future for the organization. A well thought out and clearly articulated vision would not only motivate and energize the organization, but also infuse excitement and emotion into employees to do their best to achieve the objective.

United Nations Resident Coordinator in China, Siddharth Chatterjee, said it well in a recent LinkedIn post. For businesses, "profit should not come from creating the world's problems but from solving them."

IMPLICATION

All leaders, no matter their level in an organization, have the responsibility to develop a vision for the organizations they lead. A well-crafted vision can support the objective of the larger organization but also at the same time help guide their teams around daily tasks. A vision provides clarity of direction, which is crucial in order to inspire the team at a personal and emotional level.

LEADERSHIP EXERCISE

Develop a vision statement for the team of which you are already a part. Ensure the vision statement for the team resonates with the team members but also aligns with the overall organization objective.

CHAPTER 7

MAINTAIN LONG-TERM FOCUS IN A SHORT-TERM WORLD

Long-term success requires faith—faith that our efforts to plan and execute the process will lead to the desired outcome.

—TONY DUNGY

After spending twelve years with the Minnesota Timberwolves with success, but without achieving the ultimate goal of the NBA championship, Kevin Garnett cemented his legacy with the legendary Boston Celtics basketball team in 2007–08 by leading the Celtics to their first NBA championship since 1986. However, more than Garnett's leadership presence on the court was his impact on the team off the court. Despite playing only six seasons in Boston, he will live on forever in Celtics lore. Garnett didn't only demand excellence out of his former Celtics teammates, his influence remains strong in Boston's locker room nearly a decade after leaving the organization.

That much was made clear when he paid a visit to the locker room before a game in 2022, when the Celtics made it to the NBA finals (Leger 2022). "You all know KG. He's going to bring the energy no matter what he's doing," one of the leaders on the current Celtics team, Marcus Smart, said. "That's what he's about. To play your tail off, work hard for years, and be recognized in that way is everything."

Basketball games are no doubt measured by wins or losses on the court. The championship is everything the players are playing for. Yet their leadership impact can last long after the games are over.

While technology and analytics are unlocking unprecedented opportunities for growth in the sports industry, the irony is that there are no metrics or statistics that can truly show the importance of off-the-court leadership impact.

Likewise, that is also true when we measure the impact of leaders for business or organizations in terms of delivering short-term results vs. creating long-term impacts. Quarterly earnings and yearly performance can be measured by numbers while the long-term impact can only be demonstrated long after the fact. As an example, there is still an ongoing debate about Jack Welch, former CEO of General Electric (GE), once considered one of the best business leaders in the twentieth century. His legacy is increasingly questioned not only for his ruthless management style, but also his strategic decision leading to over-reliance on GE Capital's financial services, which sowed some of the seeds for GE's near demise twenty years later (Stewart 2017, Hutchinson 2020).

During my last assignment at ExxonMobil before my retirement, one of my managers often talked about the so-called "two presidents test". What he described was that initiatives in the organization needed to be tested through two future business presidents. Only initiatives that could survive after two presidents truly demonstrate their longevity and value.

Many corporations, including ExxonMobil where I spent many years, tend to move managers around very often, especially at the leadership level. Every new executive would naturally initiate changes for a variety of reasons. While it is fundamentally a healthy practice in order to prevent an organization or business from becoming stale, frequent changes of management also create the question of how to hold leaders accountable for decisions they make in the long-term.

Adam Smith's "invisible hand," a theory he developed during the eighteenth-century Scottish enlightenment, has been the bedrock which drove the American economy and propelled the United States to the pinnacle of world economic power. The one glaring missing component from Smith's invisible hand theory and the derived company valuation methodology is how fast those invisible hands would work. As a result, leaders often struggle with the balance between delivering short-term results with long-term implication.

On the one hand, businesses and organizations need to develop long-term vision and strong, persistent culture to ensure sustainable success. Kongō Gumi in Osaka, Japan, claimed to be the world's oldest company established in 578 AD, is still in the same construction business using ancient architectural design and construction methods after fifteen hundred years (Edwards 2020). While it is a rarity, companies need to have long-term vision to drive company culture and to develop capabilities in order to sustain long-term success.

In a recent article by Yoshihiko Takubo, dean of GLOBIS University, the largest business graduate school in Japan, the author credits "customer first, value placed on people, respect for local, and lawfulness" as the reasons for the longevity of many Japanese companies. Takubo summarized in the article that "the oldest companies in the world respect traditional values often overlooked by newer firms, and much of that means valuing people" (Takubo 2022).

Arie de Geus, the man who introduced the revolutionary concept of the learning organization, revealed the key for a long and prosperous life of organizations in his 2002 book *The Living Company: Habits for Survival in a Turbulent Business Environment* (de Geus 2002), "Companies die because their managers focus on the economic activity of producing goods and services, and they forget that their organizations' true nature is that of a community of humans."

Many public companies in the United States are forced to operate to meet the quarterly earnings expectations from Wall Street, sometimes at the expense of long-term investments, especially in the context of the ongoing debate about value for shareholders vs. stakeholders. Studies often attribute the declining average life of S&P 500 companies, being about ninety years in 1935 to the current about seventeen years, to the speed of technology change and market dynamics (Handscomb and Thaker 2018, Hillenbrand et al. 2019). However, one must wonder about the impact of leadership culture created by an emphasis on the short-term vs. the long-term on the longevity of businesses.

Is longevity an objective or is creative destruction a natural selection process for deliberately dismantling established processes in order to make way for improved methods of production? For society at large, the more things destroyed by innovation the better off the society is. The more innovation is rewarded, the faster the society is replacing the old with the new. The question is who is going to survive? Are you going to be the one that gets destroyed or are you going to continue innovating out of the disruption process?

During the mid-eighties, when Japanese firms started making memory chips cheaper and better, many American companies went under, and Intel could have been one of them. Legendary Intel CEO Andy Grove's book *Only the Paranoid Survive* described this shift as the strategic inflection point (Grove 1999).

Andy Grove and Gordon Moore recalled the following conversation in their NPR interview on April 6, 2012 (Sydell 2012).

Grove says he and Moore were in his cubicle, "sitting around ... looking out the window, very sad." Then Grove asked Moore a question.

"What would happen if somebody took us over, got rid of us—what would the new guy do?" he said.

"Get out of the memory business," Moore answered.

Grove agreed. And he suggested they be the ones to get Intel out of the memory business.

They proceeded with the plan by laying off more than one third of the workforce, shutting down plants, but at the same time beefed up something that had been a side business—the microprocessor. The rest is history. Intel, at its peak in 2017, held 82.5 percent market share in an $85B microprocessor industry.

For public or non-profit organizations, it is sometimes ironically even more difficult to measure or balance the long-term vs. short-term impact.

I remember a meeting I attended in early 2000 between Mr. Paul Norris, then CEO of W.R. Grace, where I was working at the time, and Mr. Richard Roca, the newly appointed director of the Applied Physics Laboratory. APL, with seventy-one hundred employees, is the nation's largest university affiliated research center, and it "provides US government agencies with deep expertise in specialized fields to support national priorities and technology development programs."

During the meeting, Mr. Roca acknowledged the early struggle he had in order to articulate the purpose or strategic objective for APL in a clear way. What he had to cope with was the transition from a business environment where creating and growing shareholder values are the main objectives to working in a public institution like APL where the organizational objective was neither growth nor profit.

Richard Roca went on to serve as the director of APL for ten years, from 2000 to 2010, after a thirty-year career with AT&T

Bell including vice president of the storied Bell Laboratories. Based on what I learned during my research for this book, Mr. Richard Roca spent about the first three months on the job simply listening. He met his sponsors, program managers, APL management, and staff. The meeting I attended was apparently part of the outreach effort since the W.R. Grace headquarters were located very close to APL. He listened for insights into how APL should determine its success. During our discussion, he pondered aloud that the business was always looking for growth. Should APL look for diversification beyond the traditional fields? Or fundamentally, how should APL define and measure its organization's purpose?

After soul searching with the organization, his leadership team aligned that "success for APL meant making critical contributions to critical sponsor challenges." I recently checked the APL website twenty-two years after that meeting. The front page stated its purpose is "to make critical contributions to critical challenges. At APL, we feel it is our responsibility to try to solve these national challenges with the full measure of our dedication and expertise." (Johns Hopkins APL 2022)

While it is very subjective to measure the success of the organization in terms of meeting certain objectives, APL's goal of "making critical contributions to critical challenges" was soon put to the test on September 11, 2001. APL fast tracked many of its security programs in response to the terrorist attack and expanded focus on a fuller range of emerging national security challenges. Roca brought strategic vision and ability to the laboratory and guided the lab through a decade of rapidly changing circumstances by making critical contributions to critical challenges.

The fact the organization's purpose he helped define twenty years ago is still the same today, through the 9/11 terrorist attack, the 2008 financial crisis, and the rapidly changing global environment, is testimony of the impact of leadership on the long-term culture of the organization.

In summary, long-term goals are about planning for the future. It is true for either the organization or the individual. They will keep the organization energized and employees motivated. They will also give direction for leadership's decision-making. There is no one way to define the long-term impact, but one should always have a focus so that you can articulate with clarity the alignment between short-term deliverables with the long-term objectives of the organization.

IMPLICATION

For aspiring leaders, one should always have the mental clarity on what the short-term objectives vs. long-term impact you try to create as an individual as well as for your organization.

LEADERSHIP EXERCISE

As an exercise, make a list of your short-term deliverables and write out how successful completion of the short objectives would benefit the long-term vision for you as an individual, and also the long-term strategic objectives of the organization.

CHAPTER 8

BETWEEN YOUR DREAMS AND REALITY IS ACTION

———

Leadership is the capacity to translate vision into reality.

—*WARREN BENNIS*

Andy Grove was one of the most influential business thinkers in the nineties who led the transformation of Intel and created the concept of the "strategic inflection point" in business change. Yet his most powerful lessons have been what he's done. Here are some of the insights he shared with four hundred Intel executives at a speech on November 14, 2005, a year after he stepped down as the chairman of Intel (Tedlow 2006).

"In a single word, strategy is action. Strategy is not what we say, strategy is what we do. Be quick and dirty." he said, "Engage and then plan. And get it better."

One of the challenges facing many aspiring leaders is decision-making. You often hear people afraid of making decisions because they do not want to be held accountable for the wrong decisions. Sometimes, we choose willful blindness and hope that the problem will somehow quietly evaporate. This is especially true for new leaders. Unfortunately, or fortunately, we need to make decisions all the time, ranging from trivial issues like what to have for dinner, right up to life-changing decisions like who to marry or what job to take. In an advertisement by Microsoft for its To Do product, they claim that adults make about thirty-five thousand decisions in a day.

In a large organization, it is very easy for managers to default to a mindset of asking for more information when they are faced with difficult decisions, as if more information will magically make the decision easier. In addition, many organizations find themselves struggling against their own bureaucratic processes which create layers after layers of permission and ownership.

In their book *Working Backwards*, Colin Bryar and Bill Carr described the struggle Jeff Bezos was dealing with as Amazon grew in size when he realized people "were spending more time coordinating and less time building." That is when Bezos implemented the "single-threaded leadership" model to untangle dependencies so teams can work independently (Bryar and Carr 2021).

A single-threaded leader is an individual wholly dedicated to solving one business problem. The person is not only 100 percent dedicated but also accountable to a specific product, responsible for turning strategy into real results. At the same time, they are also empowered to do so.

COMPLEX VS. COMPLICATED PROBLEMS

Of course, not all business problems can be neatly directed into specific problems. In his book, *It's Not Complicated: The Art and Science of Complexity in Business,* Rick Nason explained the fundamental difference between complex world and complicated world in terms of decision-making (Nason 2017). For complicated problems, the traditional approach is to compartmentalize problems and develop solutions to the smaller problems. The expectation is that integration of the solutions to the smaller problems will lead to the overall solution. Many technical or engineering problems are solved with such an analytical approach. He defines "complex" problems as ones that are full of paradoxes that don't resolve. What works for complicated problems does not necessarily work for complex problems.

Complicated problem solving can often be codified and systematized. However, solving real-world complex problems by using tools for complicated problems can not only slow down progress but paralyze organizations in terms of decision-making. Leaders must find new, creative approaches for such problems. More importantly, organizations have to create the appropriate leadership culture for empowering decision-making at the appropriate level to create agility for the ever-changing dynamic world.

As the engineering problems extend into the social space, the complicated problems often become complex problems which are nonlinear in nature with randomness, loss of control and often interconnected and interdependent. While most leaders love the predictability and get a rush from being in control; there has to be a different leadership paradigm for simplified solutions to complex problems by focusing on insights, actions, by learning through doing. For complex business problems, leadership in creating vision is more important than ever in driving actions. Leaders often need to focus on actions in a timely manner, rather than more studies, due to unpredictability of the dynamic nature of the business world.

EMPOWERMENT FOR DECISION-MAKING

In his famous book, *Team of Teams,* Retired US Army General Stanley McChrystal studied extensively the needs for decision-making in a complex world. General McChrystal shared a beautiful example of how an orchestra was able to perform without a conductor. "Empowerment is a product of leadership." For interested readers, General McChrystal's book is a wonderful book to read and digest (McChrystal et al. 2015).

In a complex environment, the traditional hierarchical organizational model no longer works. Important things happen in the bottoms of the organization and people there need to be empowered to make decisions. For empowered execution to occur, leaders need to leverage technology and provide, not just information, but also the context of the information, down to the organization they need to make the decisions.

A working environment that empowers employees has been shown to not only improve employee job satisfaction and loyalty, but also improve decision making by inspiring employees to engage in more critical and creative thinking. Why is it so difficult to have a truly empowered working environment?

First of all, there is a misconception that empowerment simply means "giving people the power to make decisions," rather than the concept of trusting people already have the knowledge and abilities to make those decisions themselves.

Second, empowering employees requires that company and management be committed to continuous employee development, including the appropriate training and development opportunities for the employees to learn and grow.

Third, empowerment means fostering an environment of trust and helping employees learn from successes and analyze failures. Trust is a two-way street. Empowering employees means trusting them, but it also requires that they trust you, too. By doing so, there will be a sense of shared risk and responsibilities. Empowerment does not mean managers abdicate all responsibility and accountability for decision-making. Failure to support decisions publicly and stand behind your employees when employees are blamed or punished for decisions will very quickly negate any credibility and empowerment in the eyes of the employees.

Finally, managers might be afraid of losing control of situations by allowing employees more power and autonomy. In reality, effective managers know real power comes only through empowering those around you, specifically those that work for you.

Empowerment is important in all organizations, but how to apply empowerment has to be thoughtful. In an engagement I had with a McKinsey consultant, he summarized that successful empowerment required the following conditions: clarity of intent, capability, accountability, and boundary conditions. In other words, the team needs to understand not only the specific task but also context and the linkage with the overall business objective. The team needs to have not only the resources and capabilities but also feel accountable rather than being micromanaged. Finally, there should be guardrails for any teams to function effectively.

In summary, empowerment is not simply a buzzword. It is all about trust, time, communication and recognizing the potential of employees. By doing so, empowerment will increase the capacity of individuals or groups to make choices and to transform those choices into desired actions and outcomes.

DECISION-MAKING NEEDS INSIGHTS, NOT INFORMATION

"The world cannot be understood without numbers. But the world cannot be understood with numbers alone."

This quote from the book *Factfulness* by Hans Rosling is a powerful reminder of decision-making. In an increasingly digitalized world, we are all bombarded by more information and numbers (Rosling et al. 2020).

In *Factfulness*, Rosling cited a conversation he had with Pascoal Mocumbi, the prime minister of Mozambique at the time.

When the author asked the prime minister about the economic statistics for his country, the prime minister said, "I do look at those figures, but they are not so accurate. So I have also made it a habit to watch the marches on May 1 every year. They are a popular tradition in our country. And I look at people's feet, and what kind of shoes they have. I know that people do their best to look good on that day. I know that they cannot borrow their friend's shoes, because their friend will be out marching too. So I look. And I can see if they walk barefoot, or if they have bad shoes, or if they have good shoes. And I can compare what I see with what I saw last year."

A wise prime minister looks at the numbers, but not only at the numbers.

In a very similar episode, Mr. Li Keqiang, who was the governor of Liaoning Province in Northern China and is the current Chinese premier who I had a chance to meet in 2018 during my assignment in China, once spoke about China's economy during a dinner with the American ambassador to China, Clark Randt. Ambassador Randt reported that Mr. Li did not think that China's GDP figures were always reliable at the time and he instead focused on three different sets of data to measure his province's success: electricity consumption, bank lending, and rail cargo volume. The appearance of the memo in the press then led *The Economist* magazine and other China-watchers to employ the so-called Li Keqiang index themselves, as part of ongoing attempts to devise what was going on in China behind the official statistics.

Even in the sports world where data analytics are becoming powerful tools for many professional teams. The most successful teams still leverage data analytics as a tool by relying on experienced coaches and managers who have the insights to make key decisions.

Sometimes it just takes hard work to get the insights.

Sixty years ago, a young professor at MIT, John Little, wrote a paper on a theorem which has become widely known as the Little's Law. It was originally developed for queuing systems consisting of discrete objects but has since become the Newton's Law in supply chain management to explain relationships among inventory, flow time, and turnover because of its theoretical and practical importance. It is a timely example with all the current global supply chain disruptions due to the pandemic and geopolitical developments.

Mathematically, Little's law is stunningly simple: Lead Time = Work in Process (WIP) / Throughput Rate. For example, if a baseball ticket office receives about 240 customers per hour on average and it takes about three minutes (0.05hrs) to complete a transaction for purchasing a ticket, there would be about 240 times 0.05, or twelve people in the line on average.

One of the powerful applications of Little's Law is to bring clarity on bottlenecks for designing or operating complex operations. Little's Law has been widely used to optimize operations such as the FastPass queuing system at Disney World. Each restaurant, especially fast-food restaurants where speed is critical, has different ways of managing lines. For example, while McDonald's tends to have multiple parallel lines serving several waiting queuing lines, Panera Bread uses cashiers taking orders from one line and then you pick up food at a separate line. Others have multiple cashiers serving one queuing line. An analysis with Little's Law could often enhance both efficiency and the customer experience.

The operation of Long Beach and LA ports, similar to many others, were hampered by the supply chain disruptions during the pandemic with many container vessels waiting at sea for a berth at the Southern California ports because terminals were so full with Asian imports that there is little room for unloading.

The following story was widely reported at the time, but here is a summary mostly based on the *Los Angeles Times* (Dean 2021).

Mr. Ryan Petersen, CEO of the freight forwarding start-up Flexport, wanted to understand the situation at the ports of Long Beach and Los Angeles. So he rented a boat and personally observed the operations up close with real time insights to facilitate decision-making. Based on his insights he drew while touring the ports, it is clear he understood Little's Law well.

Mr. Peterson first determined that the crane operation for unloading was not the bottleneck. Instead, the bottleneck had shifted to a lack of yard space at the container terminals. The terminals were simply overflowing with containers, which meant they no longer had space to take in new containers either from ships or land. Paraphrasing Mr. Peterson, if the bottleneck appears somewhere due to disruption rather than intentional design, the negative feedback loop can rapidly cycle out of control unless actions are taken to expand the capacity at the new bottleneck.

It turned out that one of the reasons for the logjam at the port was drivers did not have the space to take containers off their truck chassis due to Long Beach's zoning code which restricts empty containers from being stacked more than two high in the truck yard to minimize the visual impact of industrial equipment in neighborhoods. What may have appeared naively as a shortage of trucks or drivers was more about a lack of space for containers. He shared his observations via Twitter, which got the attention of city and state officials. The city of Long Beach shortly thereafter issued an emergency order, allowing businesses to temporarily increase how high they could stack ocean containers in their lots in an effort to reduce the massive gridlock gripping the ports of Los Angeles and Long Beach.

The temporary change in Long Beach was not enough alone to solve the global supply chain issues due to the pandemic but Mr. Peterson certainly made a difference for the Long Beach port by converting information into insights and influenced the state officials by converting his insights into leadership action.

Although this is a unique case, it highlights the importance of getting insights on the ground for decision-making. Some leaders rely on their past experience to make judgments. Some rely on trusted advisers as sounding boards. In certain scenarios, it might take top leaders personally being on the ground to get a firsthand feel for the situation. Even if the information is already in the organization somewhere, it takes the right leadership to connect the dots and articulate it in the right context for leaders to enable decisions.

Each approach can have its appropriate place for making decisions, while each approach has its own potential traps as well. In the Flexport case, Mr. Peterson happens to be a supply chain expert, but in most cases, relying on your own technical expertise, especially in a large organization, can be viewed as a lack of trust in the technical experts. Leveraging past experience is fine as long as one is cognizant of how the context might be different.

GE famously does not sell its jet engines to airlines. I once managed a business many years ago when the product was also being leased rather than sold. There are different advantages and disadvantages for this business model from both the owner's and the customer's perspectives. One interesting insight was about the implications of technical support. In a typical sales model, technical support is often a cost which is hard to recoup once the product is sold. In a lease model, when the product is leased, technical support becomes a critical factor for helping the customer to achieve product longevity while at the same time generating additional revenue for the owner. Once you gain that insight, it is easy to make the decision on whether to enhance the technical support team.

In a *New York Times* investigative report by Michael Kimmelman on June 14, 2022, it was shown that Houston, the nation's fourth largest city, with one of the highest per capita homeless counts in the country a decade ago, made remarkably more progress than other major cities in the United States on the contentious and difficult issue of "homelessness." The number of people deemed homeless in the Houston region had been cut by 63 percent since 2011.

The report cited the key success factor was that many stake-holders, private or public, conservative or liberal, all agreed on an insight based on economic research that "housing subsidies are the most attractive policy for reducing homelessness." With that insight, the city of Houston succeeded "by teaming with county agencies and persuading scores of local service providers, corporations and charitable non-profits to row in unison" by sharing goals and information, rather than competing for federal funds and duplicating services. With leadership from the city, all parties came together for the "housing first" initiative.

In most cases, senior leaders have a few trusted advisors to provide first-hand information and insights without being filtered through layers of bureaucratic processes. However, it also requires organizations to have a psychologically safe and transparent culture.

MAKING DECISIONS IS EASY

"Making a decision is easy while the key is to stick with the decision. The more you stick with the decision, the better the decision becomes." This is a quote from a dinner conversation I had with the president of a major multinational company a few years ago. While the statement may at first sound self-serving, it was truly an aha moment for me.

Making business decisions may seem especially hard for people with technical backgrounds who are trained to seek the truth as if everything in the business world has THE RIGHT answer. Some people put off making decisions by endlessly searching for further information, while others defer to other people to offer recommendations.

You have heard the saying that the only thing worse than making the wrong decision is not making a decision at all. The problem is you think you have time when, in reality, time is of the essence for most business decisions in a dynamic and fast-moving business environment.

Here are some perspectives to ease the decision-making process:

First of all, your decision is unlikely THE final decision. Just think about a chess game played on sixty-four small squares. In just the first four moves, there are 308 different ways to play. Just think about the countless possibilities along the way, and no one is able to predict what's going to happen next, which I think is the true beauty of our world. In most cases, you must play in order to unleash the unknown possibilities of life.

While we may believe that this is the final decision about some issue, most decisions are rarely those involving life and death. We often tend to overdramatize the consequences of each decision. This decision will most likely lead to other "forks in the road" and opportunities for change. In other words, one should always maintain a healthy perspective that even though it may not seem likely, this single decision will not affect humanity as we know it. Appreciate the power of serendipity and that things often have a way of working themselves out.

Second, all business decisions are made with incomplete information. The world is constantly changing. While sound decisions do require the right level of available information, we also need to acknowledge that almost all business decisions will need to be made with incomplete information.

Finally, for making personal decisions, your intuition is probably telling you more. The key is to take the effort in seeking and understanding your inner self to understand how your values affect your decision-making. As we discussed in an early part of the book, having clarity in your leadership values and purpose can guide you in making difficult decisions in challenging times.

Your specific goals may change, but your values are deeply embedded principles which will guide you on the right path. Author Deepak Chopra once said, "The universe has no fixed agenda. Once you make a decision, it works around that decision. There is no right or wrong, only a series of possibilities that shift with each thought, feeling and action you experience."

In the business world, decisiveness is key to effectively executing plans and achieving goals. Leaders need to be willing to take charge and not shirk from decisions, especially during difficult times. It is important to balance the costs of continuing to deliberate, gathering information, and delaying a decision vs. the costs of making a poor choice. Decisiveness instills confidence and creates clarity for organizations.

OPPORTUNITY COST VS. SUNK COST

Opportunity cost and sunk cost are two important economic concepts which often affect how businesses make decisions. When you say yes to anything, you are explicitly or implicitly saying no to something else. You can only handle so many things in life at the same time.

Opportunity cost is what you give up when you choose an option and can no longer pursue the other option. The key to minimize opportunity cost is by choosing the option that benefits the most vs. the next best alternative. Sunk cost is an expense that is already gone. You have already paid for it, and you can't get it back. The key is not to let sunk cost have too much influence on your decisions for the future.

Conceptually, the numbers of opportunity costs and sunk costs are almost limitless, but in the context of individual decisions or business decisions, they would generally include money, time, or effort. The concepts, while mostly used in an economic sense for business or investment decisions, are equally applicable to many personal decisions.

The general observation is that we human tend to give too much attention to sunk costs and not enough focus on opportunity costs when making decisions. This is true for businesses as well as individuals. In reality, decision-making should focus on the future, not the past. Though the past can teach us a lot, the past is gone and won't come back. Don't forfeit future benefits to justify a past decision. Leverage your energy for future opportunity rather than worrying about the past.

For business decisions, opportunity cost informs business decisions in several dimensions.

First of all, in a business world where resources are always limited, business strategy is not just about the importance of what you do, but more about clarity of what you do not do. Opportunity cost brings a sharp focus on to the decisions you make vs. the next best alternative. People often focus on the proposed action vs. doing nothing, which most often is not the benchmark one should be comparing against.

Second, opportunity cost analysis also helps create business urgency for making a decision, which is even more important in a dynamic business environment. When the opportunity cost is high, expediting decision-making is often better than continued information gathering and analysis to perfection. On the other hand, if you are limited by available opportunities and the opportunity cost is low, the pursuit of your business objectives should be more persistent.

Very often you hear statements such as "the system does not really work, but we already made the investment" or "we already paid for it, we might as well go for it." The hardest things to let go of are things emotionally attached to decisions you already made. The more time or money you have invested in a person, product, or idea, the harder it is to move on. It is not just about individual decisions. Businesses have an extremely difficult time killing bad projects. Investors often hold onto stocks which have lost significant value and hope they will somehow recover the loss even when there are better investment options.

I will end with a quote from Peter Drucker, "Wherever you see a successful business, someone once made a courageous decision."

IMPLICATION

Strategy is action. Strategy is not what we say, strategy is what we do. In the business world, decisiveness is key to effectively executing plans and achieving goals. Leaders need to be willing to take charge and not shirk from decisions, especially during difficult times.

LEADERSHIP EXERCISE

Identify one business or personal decision that you need to make in the near future. Ask yourself if you are delaying making the decision simply because you are afraid of making the wrong decision or you genuinely believe you would have better insights for a better decision later, even considering the opportunity cost.

CHAPTER 9

WHY A TINY ROPE CAN HOLD AN ELEPHANT

A Leader is best when people barely know he exists, when his work is done, his aim fulfilled, they will say: we did it ourselves.

—*LAO TZU*

When I started writing the book, I set up a leadership survey, which I will discuss in Chapter 18. As part of the survey, I asked people to share their personal leadership stories. The following is a personal but powerful story shared to me by Srini Karra, a former colleague.

> *While growing up in Southern India, whenever I visited a temple, the sight of a huge elephant tied up with a small rope always amazed me! On the other side, seeing elephants pulling tons of wooden logs, causing mayhem in tens of acres of sugarcane fields, kept me perplexed about how they can be restrained with a tiny rope at the temple. Later I realized the elephant is the potential in oneself and the tiny rope is the imaginary*

constraints one constantly experiences, which makes them 'powerless.' Ever since, I started working with teams around me to bring clarity around strengths, opportunities, objectives, and purpose in general. Enjoyed winning through others!

Elephants could obviously break away from the tiny rope any time, but they are conditioned from when they are very young to believe they cannot break away. As a result, they are stuck right where they are. How often in our lives have we been hampered by those imaginary constraints and fears? It's only when we admit our fears and recognize how those imaginary constraints are holding us back that we can begin moving forward.

EMPOWERMENT AND OWNERSHIP

Empowerment has become a buzzword in the business world and is widely used in many contexts. Working environment that empowers employees has been shown to not only improve employee job satisfaction and loyalty but also improve decision-making by inspiring employees to engage in more critical and creative thinking. However, it is often very difficult to have a truly empowered working environment, partly because of some of the misconceptions about empowerment we had discussed in Chapter 8.

From the perspective of aspiring leaders who are seeking empowerment, it is very critical to understand and internalize that empowerment requires you to take ownership of issues, rather than "waiting to be empowered". You need to be proactive in participating in the decision-making processes that concern your well-being, your own rights, either in the business environment or broad society context. The question you should ask yourself is not who is going to let you, but rather who is going to stop you.

In a video posted by the CEO of Panera Bread, Mr. Niren Chaudhary, he describes the culture he was trying to create at Panera Bread, "own it." He went on to explain that when you own it, you always talk in the language of solution. Many people can bring problems. When you own it, you bring solutions along with the problems. Mr. Chaudhary emphasized it was okay when people bring problems for the purpose of informing, discussing, and brainstorming. But we should avoid bringing only problems if the focus is to simply complain.

In the context of empowerment, "owning one's endeavor, is a step towards self-actualization, aligned with self-awareness that yields curiosity, continuous learning, and understanding, along an evolving journey of the servant, where leadership is implicit," said Sebastian Thalanany in a comment on one of my leadership blogs about the Panera Bread culture.

While it's important to demonstrate ownership by bringing solutions, that doesn't mean you should go as far as the popular phase "don't bring me problems, bring me solutions." While the idea is well-intentioned to empower teams for problem-solving, this dichotomy does not always create the right leadership culture. While it is true a problem is about negativity while a solution brings positivity, feeding organizations with complaints and negative emotions creates negative energy in organizations. This mindset can shut down employees and create a culture of fear which prevents people from surfacing hidden problems early before they become full-blown crises. Organizations need to strive for a culture of openness so that people can bring forward problems and work together for solutions.

Many Western businesses today operate as global business units. Headquarters often makes strategic decisions and local teams in different parts of the world simply implement the strategy. This naturally creates a tug-of-war between the two different centers of gravity. On the one hand, the team at headquarters often feels that they have the strategic view of the overall business strategy, while the local teams tend to believe they know what it takes to win in the local market with local customers. It is similar to the typical tension between marketing and sales teams in many organizations. It is an ever more prominent issue for large markets such as China or India for global companies, at least partly due to the culturally different business environments.

There is no one simple answer to the right decision-making process or organizational structure. The specifics for each organization will have to dictate the right organization models. However, each model would also drive very different leadership behavior and organization culture.

During my assignment in China to lead ExxonMobil's capital investment project, we worked with the consulting group started by General Stanley McChrystal to facilitate the "Team of Teams" concept in order to have more effective teamwork between the headquarters team and the local teams in China. It was during those discussions that I suddenly realized that the proper translation for the word "empowerment" simply did not exist in Chinese. It is often translated to something along the lines of "permission" which has a very different connotation in English. It is partly a reflection of the culture not only in China, but in many East Asian countries. While employees in the West are typically looking for independence from their bosses and "ownership" of their jobs, trying to empower employees in China with the same mindset often gets the opposite of what you expect.

During my interview with Keith Hartsfield, executive vice president and chief product officer of iRobot, he recalled his experience when he was with Motorola managing a team in China. He told me that he traveled to China on a regular basis to work with his team, but the dynamic did not start as he had expected.

"But when I got there, it was like this. I was the big boss who's supposed to tell everybody what to do. And the first couple of months they were really worried because I was not telling them what to do. I was asking them all these questions, and they weren't used to sharing what they actually thought."

This reaction is not uncommon among newly arrived Western executives in China. He wasn't wrong to try to empower his employees. But he didn't appreciate that Chinese culture and history work to prevent employees from taking advantage of empowerment when it's offered to them where there is a natural tendency of deference to authority.

First of all, the culture of deference to authority often makes employees hunker down until they can figure out what's really on the boss's mind, rather than thinking and acting independently for action.

In addition, employees in those environments also tend to be fearful of making mistakes, especially with a new leader or in a new working environment. They worry about inadvertently straying too far from where the leader wants them to be, and they see risk in asking questions that might make them appear ignorant and expose them to painful criticism. Although the younger generations, who have been exposed to the Western working culture, are becoming increasingly vocal, many still tend to be reticent in the workplace.

In order to encourage and energize the team, Hartsfield spent a lot of personal time with the team members in order to establish trust and get to know them at a personal level. Eventually they "loosened up and I started to understand what they thought it would take to succeed? What they thought success would look like? Because my definition was different from theirs in many cases."

"Eyes on, hands off" is how one of my former colleagues, Dr. Prasanna Joshi, succinctly described empowerment in a comment on one of my blog posts about empowerment. While empowerment is important in most workplaces, there are cultural quirks unique to any workplace. Positive leaders need to be ready to assess and adjust their approach to empowerment with every unique situation.

EMPOWERMENT AND SELF-ACTUALIZATION

Empowerment is important in a work context, but the concept of empowerment is much broader. Empowerment is really about a partnership valuing self and others, freedom to make choices, but also to accept responsibility.

For example, empowerment of women is considered important in order to achieve gender equality globally, especially in many developing countries where women are traditionally discriminated against.

I recently had a conversation with Ms. Ananya Jain, who grew up in Jammu, India and had a difficult childhood due to her family situation. With the support from her mother, she was able to develop a fiercely independent mindset to pursue her interests from a very young age. At the age of fourteen, she received an award from the President of India for her work on bio fertilizer. She has subsequently been recognized by other organizations, including the Swiss government.

When I asked Ananya about the sources of her inspiration and courage that helped her to take control of her situation, she repeatedly brought up the strong influence of her mother on her directly and indirectly.

I think a lot of that came from my mom, because my mom went through a really ugly divorce with my father. And very quickly, I saw that she had little or no control over her finances when they were getting divorced. And I saw the immense amount of courage that she had to have in the Indian legal system to come out on the other side, support both herself, my education in the US and then my sister.

And I think it is her courage to sit up and take control of her life as a child that I observed and that helped me make up my own mind about not wanting to be in control by someone else or situation. So that was the inspiration. But I think specifically for me how that manifested is: I said, I never want to be financially dependent on a company or person ever again, because I can see how much that binds you to something.

That fierce independence empowered her to set a goal for the next fifteen years to find financial independence. She had a vision of "creating something that was joyous for not just me, but for people around me, a company where my employees feel like they're financially free and empowered, make decisions for themselves while they're in my company, and even when they leave to join another employer. [...] I don't look back and think, hey, in my quest to be financially free, and financially joyous, I left other people hollow."

With that mindset, when she graduated from Georgia Tech with an engineering degree, Ananya Jain founded FullCircle LLC, a global mental health technology start-up, which has attracted wide attention, including being the recipient of the prestigious The Diana Award from the Royal Family of the UK for her work in creating disruptive technology for mental health.

She and her co-founders want to make an impact on the mental health of Gen Z with technology or approaches that better resonate with the younger generations. They want to have "an uplifting tone in mental healthcare, a flexible approach, and better communities—especially in a COVID era where social interactions are quite frankly, largely on social media."

While one's mission can be large or small, the key to empowerment is self-actualization. Introduced by psychologist Abraham Maslow in 1962 as the highest level of Maslow's hierarchy of needs, self-actualization can be defined as the realization or fulfillment of one's talent and potential, a drive present in everyone.

Yiying Lu, an artist or artrepreneur as she preferred to be called, shared with me her endeavor for the creation of a dumpling emoji. As someone who was born and raised in Shanghai, lived in China, Australia, the United Kingdom, and the United States, she has developed many interests including art, design, and food. While she was texting with her friend Jennifer Lee on an iPhone in August 2015, she realized that there was no emoji representing her beloved dumpling. Most of us would have just used the word and stopped there. Here is how the story unfolded based on what Yiying shared with me and a story reported by *Fast Company* (McCracken 2017).

"Well, I'm a designer. I have imagination. Maybe I can do something about it." She told herself. "Designing emoji wasn't my job. It wasn't my career. … but I kind of just took the responsibility."

She proceeded with not only a dumpling emoji design but went on a mission with her friend Jennifer to incorporate a dumpling into the emoji system, though at the time they had no idea where to start. It turns out that a new emoji would require the approval of the Unicode Consortium, an industrial consortium responsible for consistent encoding and display of textual characters. It is fair to say that including dumplings on the list was probably not their highest priority.

Yiying and Jennifer went on a mission by personally attending the Unicode Consortium conference, and Jennifer got herself onto the Emoji subcommittee. In March 2017, the Unicode Consortium officially announced Emoji Version 5.0 with the dumpling emoji design 🥟 as one of the fifty-six new additions.

Through this effort, Yiying also realized that "dumpling is actually universal. Georgia has khinkali. Japan has gyoza. Korea has mandu. Italy has ravioli. Polish people have pierogi. Russian people have pelmeni. Argentina has empanadas. Jewish people have kreplach. Chinese people have potstickers and various other dumplings. Tibet and Nepal have momos. Turkish people have manti."

A small dumpling emoji is now available for people to use around the world through the leadership of Yiying and Jennifer. Since then, Yiying also designed the official Unicode emoji of the Boba tea 🧋, the Chinese takeout box 🥡, the fortune cookie 🥠, chopsticks 🥢, and the peacock 🦚.

In summary, empowerment is not simply a buzzword. It is all about trust and about recognizing the potential of employees. It is about knowing ourselves better and becoming stronger and powerful within ourselves. By doing so, empowerment will increase the capacity of individuals or groups to make choices and to transform those choices into desired actions and outcomes.

For aspiring leaders, you must be ready to empower yourself to pursue goals and objectives aligned with your values, regardless of your situations, rather than waiting to be empowered. The power of a free society is to provide that environment for people to explore, try, and learn, but you have to be willing to empower yourself.

It is especially important to be cognizant of the cultural context of empowerment in today's global business environment. Be present as the team goes through the beginning steps of a project so that members can see firsthand what empowerment really means. Leaders should be willing to spend time with the team together to mentor and coach how empowerment can unlock employees' ideas for business successes, at the same time, unleash their potential in order to truly achieve the goal for empowerment for their leadership development.

I will end with a quote from Ms. Rose Hall, senior vice president of AXA XL and head of construction innovation. When she was asked about advice for women to achieve more successes in the construction industry. "Say yes first and then figure out how!" was her answer. My advice is to be thoughtful but always bias toward action.

Don't let the tiny rope on the elephant become a constraint in what you should pursue and what you could achieve.

IMPLICATION

Empowerment requires you to take ownership of issues, rather than "waiting to be empowered." Do not let imaginary constraints and fears hamper you or hold you back from your true potential to do great things.

LEADERSHIP EXERCISE

Identify something at your workplace that you have always wished would get done but has not happened for whatever reasons. Identify two imaginary constraints which are stopping you from making it happen.

Develop a specific plan to overcome the constraints.

CHAPTER 10

INCLUSION STARTS WITH SELF-ACCEPTANCE

—

Wanting to be someone else is a waste of the person you are.

—MARILYN MONROE

Spring is a beautiful time in Texas, and I often see many wildflowers along the walking paths. Those flowers are pretty and graceful, but often unremarkable and insignificant. They generally do not stand out as anything extraordinary. In fact, most people walk past them without even noticing their presence. Being an amateur photographer, I tend to carry a mental picture frame and occasionally photograph some when I have my camera with me. As I was going through some of the photos, I noticed two things. First of all, even though most flowers are common species, each flower is unique and beautiful in its own way if you are willing to get a closeup focused view. Second, each individual flower may not stand out, but putting them together can create a beautiful portfolio.

We need to constantly remind ourselves that each one of us is unique and different. Each one of us has personality traits and skills that will enable us to contribute to business and society in a positive way. Unless we are willing to focus on the individual and pay close attention, we will probably miss their uniqueness and individuality. In addition, while recognizing that businesses have standards and companies have culture, let's not lose sight of the fact that the world is a better place because of our individuality. Our similarities make us strong, but our differences make us stronger. Likewise, the richness created by diverse perspectives of ideas normally results in better decisions and better business results.

As individuals, we all have to start with self-awareness. Inclusion and belonging start with self-acceptance. We have to first have the belief that we belong in order to give us the courage to be authentic, be transparent, and even be vulnerable. Regardless of our background or culture, we should be respectful toward people from other cultures, but also be proud of the traditions or cultures we grow up with. Culture can mean people from a different part of the world, or simply a different part of the same town. Only then can we expect to be included in whatever organizations or community we seek to belong.

At the same time, we all view the world through our own lens. We must be vigilant about the fact that each lens creates a different image and can influence how we experience the world. The individual experience could either limit or encourage us to seek to confirm evidence and make us hold on to our mental models and convictions. Each time we have a new experience, we add a new lens to the perspective of how we see the world.

While each one of us, by nature, sees the world with a perspective different from others, we also want to see the world through other's eyes, imagine with other's imagination at the same time as with our own.

Just like photography, where we need to have closeup focus, the same approaches can be applied in daily life or the business world. Focus on the unique capabilities and characters of an individual person. Find the extraordinary in the ordinary. Rather than settling for people who fit in the culture, search for people who can enrich the culture.

DIVERSITY IS A FACT BUT INCLUSION IS A CHOICE

You may have noticed that some people, more than others, tend to feel chilly in the air-conditioned offices.

Thermal comfort is calculated based on energy balance. If the heat leaving the occupant is greater than the heat entering the occupant, the thermal perception is "cold." If the heat entering the occupant is greater than the heat leaving the occupant, the thermal perception is "warm" or "hot." The mathematical calculation involved is based on the average characteristics of an individual person, as many systems tend to be. The American Society of Heating, Refrigerating and Air-Conditioning Engineers officially codified it (Belluck 2015).

The problem is there is no such thing as an average person. According to the Centers for Disease Control and Prevention (CDC), the average height for American men is about five feet, nine inches while the average height for Asian women is about five feet, two inches. Taking into consideration the differences in size, one study concluded the neutral temperature for Japanese women was 77.36 degrees Fahrenheit while it was 71.78 for European and North American males (Cha 2015, Kingma and Lichtenbelt 2015).

Since "average" in the standard was based on experiments conducted in the sixties with men, the office temperature was probably fine when most office workers were indeed men. If you look around the office today, the mix is obviously different. No wonder some feel chilly.

When I first learned about this office temperature analysis, it made me start thinking about what other potential biases are encoded in the system we all take for granted. It is still working in process but increasing numbers of organizations have passed the point that diversity was considered a business nuisance. Many take diversity as not just necessity but arguably a competitive advantage.

While the concept of diversity and inclusion is not only accepted, but embraced and celebrated in many organizations, it is still a challenge to incorporate all the elements that make an organization truly diverse. In addition, there are often biases ingrained in systems which may not be intentional or obvious. Such is the case for the office temperature setting. Here are a few facts:

- In 2000, there were two female CEOs of Fortune 500 companies. It has increased to forty-one out of five hundred in 2022. That is a whopping 2000 percent increase in twenty years, yet still well below fair representation. An analysis published by the Center for Economic Policy

Research and the World Economic Forum suggested that countries led by women had systematically and significantly better COVID-19 outcomes. A recent article in the *Financial Times* (Caulkin 2022) wondered out loud if the rise of women will go on to change the fundamentals of management from the inside.

- A similar underrepresentation is true for Asian, Hispanic and African Americans in terms of leadership positions in academic, industry, and other organizations. For example, Asians represent 10.9 percent of faculty but, again, only 2.3 percent of the university presidents in the United States in 2017, which is an improvement from 1.5 percent in 2013 (Davis and Fry 2019, Seltzer 2017).
- Many companies tend to use statistics to measure progress for diversity. Statistics are important, but they are often a lagging indicator. More important for changing workplace culture is often addressing the unconscious biases that prevent minorities from getting to leadership positions.

I have managed and worked with global teams with very diverse backgrounds and realize that diversity is still an uncomfortable topic for an open discussion for many managers and leaders. I have seen some very awkward communications about diversity throughout my career.

There are many types of biases. In the context of diversity and inclusion, we need to realize that we all have unconscious biases. TV journalist Tom Brokaw once said, "Bias, like beauty, is often in the eye of the beholder." The key is to develop the ability to leave our comfort zone, willingness to examine our assumptions, and the capacity to choose whether or not to let the harmful bias dictate our behavior.

If you are surrounded by others who share your perspectives, your career paths, and your outside interests, then it's important to understand how your bias manifests with your teams and your leadership style. Inclusive leaders need to maintain an objective and healthy perspective by tapping a wide range of different viewpoints. Informal networks are a powerful advantage for many who share the same perspectives, same interests, and same cultural background, which could potentially reenforce unconscious biases. Inclusive leaders need to be vigilant about not only how decisions are made, but also who gets heard and who gets excluded from informal discussion. We are human, and we all have natural biases. Very often, having an open mind, stepping back and challenging basic assumptions are still warranted and necessary.

After all, according to a McKinsey study (Hunt, Layton and Prince 2015), the companies in the top 25 percent in terms of gender diversity were 15 percent more likely to have financial returns that were above their national industry median, and the companies in the top 25 percent in terms of racial/ethnic diversity were 35 percent more likely to have financial returns above their national industry median.

From the perspective of aspiring leaders, especially those from under-represented backgrounds, one needs to make a conscious decision about how you want to approach such biases. There is no one right way to deal with those biases. However, we all need to recognize that biases in society are upheld by both the active and passive participation of all of us. They won't disappear by themselves unless we find ways to intervene.

Some try to deal with it at a personal level by trying to fit in. For example, there is a long history of people anglicizing their names in order to make them "fit in". I used the name "Steve" when I was in business school with the thought that it would make it easier to engage with others. However, I never really felt natural and eventually went back to my real name given by my parents. People often have to ask how to pronounce my name, and I normally take the opportunity to explain how the Chinese phonetic system works. The reality is some unconscious biases will always be there in workplace and you are going to face it.

Others deal with biases head-on, either by creating their own path or by confronting the biases directly. Malala Yousafzai, the youngest person to ever receive a Nobel Prize at the age of seventeen, chose a path very early on. Speaking with the BBC, she detailed her life in Pakistan under Taliban occupation at the age of eleven, when girls were banned from attending school. After her story was made into a *New York Times* documentary, a Taliban gunman shot her in an assassination attempt in retaliation for her activism. However, the threat on her life instead strengthened her resolve to fight not just for herself, or girls in Pakistan, but for every girl in the world. She founded the Malala Fund, which according to its website, is now working across eight different countries.

Many prefer to take the approach of "assuming good intent" in the workplace. Rather than immediately judging the other party, they choose to assume that the other party meant well or was doing their best. Most of the time, nothing good comes out of a negative response, especially when that's coupled with an equally rude reaction. Instead, the more effective approach might be to take a proactive approach to correct the situation.

Duane Kozub of Parkland Refinery shared an interesting approach as an example of how to deal with such an experience. One of his colleagues, a young female member of the leadership team, was always getting drowned out by other "louder" guys in brainstorming sessions. She was feeling discouraged from not being heard during these discussions. This was all the more important as, in many organizations, leadership readiness for aspiring leaders is often measured by our willingness and ability to speak up.

Kozub advised her to speak up by calling out the name of the loud person: "hey, Mark, what do you think about ...?" When people hear their names in a busy environment, they tend to focus their attention on whoever said their name. By using similar tactics, aspiring leaders can become more emboldened to contribute and become more confident.

In summary, we all need to recognize that we cannot avoid biases regardless of what approach we take. We will always have to deal with some unconscious biases either in the workplace or in society. The key is to have a prepared mind and intentional approach, rather than emotionally reacting to the situation in the moment. At the same time, we should also recognize and acknowledge our own unconscious biases and implement a practical approach to counteract biases through intentional behavior changes. In addition, do not fight the battle alone. Leveraging the communities who are facing similar issues is a much more powerful approach if you want to have sustainable change.

In the end, leadership is about having the self-awareness to believe that we belong in order to give us the courage to lead, and the self-conviction to create an environment for people around us to maximize their potential. Quoting leadership guru John C. Maxwell, "people don't care how much you know until they know how much you care."

IMPLICATION

Inclusion and belonging start with self-acceptance. Self-acceptance starts with self-awareness. We have to first have the belief that we belong in order to give us the courage to be authentic, be transparent, and even be vulnerable. When faced with biases, the key is to have a prepared mind and intentional approach, rather than emotionally reacting to the situation in the moment.

LEADERSHIP EXERCISE

When you choose potential mentors, do you pick people whose experience aligns with yours? Seek out a mentor with a very different background. Getting outside of your comfort zone can not only help you, but potentially help the other party as well.

CHAPTER 11

GOOD COMMUNICATION STARTS WITH LISTENING

The single biggest problem in communication is the illusion that has taken place.

— GEORGE BERNARD SHAW

The BBC reported a story a few years ago about a person who was visiting Mexico for the first time. When she asked a local ice cream street vendor when he expected a new delivery of chocolate ice cream, she was told "ahorita," which directly translates to "right now." After waiting for half an hour with no sign of the delivery, she went back and asked again and got the same answer, or almost the same answer, "ahoriiiiita" with an obvious expression of confusion from the vendor. It turns out, in Mexico, "ahorita" can either refer to the present moment, or a vague reference to some point in the future, or never. The stretch in the /i/ sound in the word "ahorita" can be a demonstration of the stretching of time (Ring 2017).

There is something special about the ambiguity in that ice-cream example. But in the business world, creating clarity in communication is increasingly becoming one of the most important skills for everyone who aspires to influence, inspire, or lead an organization or team.

One hundred and fifty years ago, on March 1, 1872, President Ulysses S. Grant signed the Yellowstone National Park Protection Act into law and the world's first national park was born. It was a crowning achievement of three separate expeditions, especially the scientific expedition in 1871 led by Ferdinand V. Hayden. The Yellowstone Act stated, "the headwaters of the Yellowstone River... is hereby reserved and withdrawn from settlement, occupancy, or sale... and dedicated and set apart as a public park or pleasuring-ground for the benefit and enjoyment of the people."

During my visit to the park early in 2022, I learned the role communication played in the success of the effort. During an era without internet or means for convenient travels, the way the expedition teams communicated the wonders of Yellowstone played a pivotal role in the successful effort in convincing Congress to act. The wonders of the Yellowstone River—shown through photographs, paintings, and sketches—captivated the imagination of Congress and propelled the establishment of the national park merely six months after the expedition led by Ferdinand V. Hayden.

The importance of communication is not just reserved for major decisions, such as the establishment of a national park, but also for daily life or business activities. Knowing your audience involves not only understanding others and their perspectives, but also ensuring they understand your words and the frames of reference you use to communicate your points and conclusions.

USE DIFFERENT LANGUAGES FOR CROSS-DISCIPLINE COMMUNICATION

During my professional career, I transitioned from being an engineer to a business manager. I have also worked with many very talented legal professionals throughout my career, but especially during my decade long stint managing a global business in technology licensing. While communication in the corporate world is always challenging, cross-discipline communication poses additional challenges.

Engineers, lawyers, consultants, and businesspeople speak fundamentally different professional languages. As a result, miscommunications or misunderstandings can and often do occur, especially when such a team has to work across the table with external parties. Communication gaps are often heightened during stressful times.

While we have to be careful to avoid over-generalizing, which can lead to stereotyping, it is true that the different training for each discipline indeed makes us think differently in terms of how we approach issues and problems.

- Businesspeople tend to focus on the bottom line and often would like to know the conclusions first. They tend to make judgments based on experience and the 80/20 rule, which asserts that 80 percent of the outcomes come from 20 percent of the causes for any given events. The approach is important in a fast-moving dynamic business environment but can come across as a lack of curiosity or patience to technical people.

- Technical people tend to focus on the logic and process which lead to the conclusions. Technical people often feel it is necessary to go through many details and the complete story for the audience to understand how the conclusion was derived but can run into the danger of getting the key messages lost in the details.

- Legal professionals are trained to think about different scenarios, but especially the worst-case scenarios. The main business issues in any contracts are typically easy to reach consensus on. However, many legal clauses in an agreement are there to provide protection for low-probability, high-consequence events. While necessary, not everyone has a good grasp of the necessity unless explained in a way people can understand. Overly focusing on those causes could create a negative dynamic when the business team needs to make things happen.

- Consultants, especially those from the large management consulting firms, mostly focus on frameworks and structures. They try to create clarity by simplifying complex business issues into simple frameworks. While it is most effective with management, with whom the big picture views will resonate, the approach does not always easily connect with technical people.

Effective leaders can speak different languages in order to work effectively with people from different disciplines. It is important to learn to understand each other's perspectives, speak each other's language, and more importantly to make intentional efforts to reduce friction in conversations. Here are some recommendations.

First of all, take a moment to think from others' perspectives. To effectively communicate, we must realize we are all different in the way we perceive the world around us. It may make perfect sense to you, but would it resonate with your counterpart? What is there in the business relationship or transaction for each party and why do they care? Otherwise, a message, which might sound very reasonable and persuasive to you, can sound foreign to the other parties. Just like the "ahorita" moment for the visitor in Mexico. Conversely, be a good listener if you are on the receiving end of any conversations. Try to ask for clarification rather than make assumptions.

Second, use language and phrases people can understand. If necessary, take the time to explain any potentially confusing phrases and words in the context of the conversation. Technical worlds are full of jargon and abbreviations people outside of the field may not have any idea what they mean. For non-lawyers, legal phrases can be intimidating and hard to understand. A study by Professor Jonah Berger at Wharton quantitatively showed that a simple shift in language could help improve customer satisfaction (Packard and Berger 2021). The paper suggests that linguistic concreteness—the tangibility, specificity, or imaginability of words employees use when speaking to customers—can shape consumer attitudes and behaviors.

Third, use examples rather than abstract concepts. When you sense the challenge in explaining something to the other party, take a step back and try to think of using examples to illustrate the point, rather than just repeating yourself. Regardless of profession, people relate to and better digest actual examples than conceptual descriptions.

Finally, it is about people. The more you get to know people, the better you can connect. Regardless of how differently we think or how we prefer to communicate, we are all human. Better communication leads to community, to understanding, to mutual respect, and, in the end, better results. The best ideas often emerge from the collision of different insights.

CROSS-CULTURAL COMMUNICATIONS

The ice cream story from Mexico is just one of many similar examples.

- The Korean language has a unique and versatile phrase " 우리 [uri]," which means "we/our" in English. Apparently, it is not always as all-inclusive as the English "we"—that is, it might not include the listeners, and it might not even be plural, especially when used to talk about family or country. Scholars believe the use is a reflection of the Korean culture's emphasis on the whole rather than the individual.

- I learned from a colleague that "kal" in Hindi could mean either yesterday or tomorrow. "Kal" is the word derived from "Kaal." Kaal is the time between sunrise to sunrise in India. As such, "kal" can be the time from today's sunrise to yesterday's or tomorrow's sunrise. The exact meaning in a sentence would be "one day away from today," but only the context will tell if it is yesterday or tomorrow.

- The Japanese language is highly contextual. This means there is an emphasis on implicit, indirect, and ambiguous communication. It is a common mistake for Western companies to return from negotiations with Japanese businesses to celebrate success, while in time it becomes apparent the Japanese are in fact not interested in doing business with you. For example, "Yes" in Japanese, "hai," is often ambiguous depending on the situation. It is used in much the same way an English speaker says "I see" without actually agreeing or disagreeing with what you just said. It's always good to double-check with someone if you think your Japanese counterpart has a question mark on his or her face.

- Likewise, there are many ambiguous expressions in Chinese which are prone to misinterpretation. For example, a phrase you hear often in business meetings is "Let's talk about it later." It could mean "let's discuss later, possibly privately" but also could mean "I am hoping we'll both forget, and it never comes up again." It's up to you to figure out the true intent based on the context or the body language.

With today's global business environment, it is not only important to have the linguistic concreteness to ensure clarity, but more importantly to have the awareness of the different cultural contexts of the people you work with. This is especially true when you have team members who work around the world and many may have anxiety about communicating in English outside of their specific business or technical context, even if they seem to speak English fluently. Even in the same culture, people with different backgrounds or in different professions may interpret the same English word very differently.

CORPORATE JARGON MEANS DIFFERENT THINGS TO DIFFERENT PEOPLE

The problem with many corporate communication cultures is the use of jargon which prevents clarity and creates misalignment. When compounded with employees working in a different culture or using a different language, the intended messages are often lost. Straightforward communications build credibility and help employees better understand not only the what but also the why. Even with a seemingly obvious choice of words, the intended message does not always come across easily.

As mentioned in Chapter 9, when I was discussing empowerment, I realized that the word "empowerment", widely used in the Western corporate world, did not have a simple translation in Chinese. Likewise, the word "Guanxi" in Chinese, often literally translated to "relationship" in English, contains much more subtext.

Communication technology, ironically, can further compound the issues of business communication. While PowerPoint was intended to facilitate business communication, it can become an impediment to clear communication in the business world. For example, many organizations, intentionally or unintentionally, place more weight on how ideas are presented rather than the credibility of the ideas. No wonder Jeff Bezos banned the use of PowerPoint in Amazon executive meetings in 2018. Instead, everyone sits silently for the first thirty minutes of executive meetings to read, a "six-page memo that is narratively structured with real sentence, topic sentence, verbs, and nouns," instead of bullet points which tend to gloss over ideas.

Advancement of information technology has made communication more efficient than ever before. Anytime, anywhere connection enables instant communication with people anytime, anywhere on the planet. At the same time, effective communication is getting more complex and difficult than ever before in the increasingly complex global business environment.

For any business initiatives to be successful, leaders must cultivate a meaningful relationship that requires clear, honest, and reciprocal communication. In addition, we should realize that electronic communication is no replacement for face-to-face communication, especially for communications between parties who just started new working relationships. After all, the landmark study by Albert Mehrabian demonstrated that 55 percent of the meaning of any message is generated by face and body. Another 38 percent is derived from the way someone speaks (tone, volume, etc.) and only the remaining 7 percent is from the actual words said (Mehrabian 1970).

This is especially important for global businesses when employees are located in different parts of the world. In the end, it is not just about policies and rules, it is about winning the hearts and minds of employees. When companies implement new initiatives or policy changes, the immediate focus of many organizations tends to be on customers, investors, and the community. Unfortunately, many organizations underestimate the importance of their own employees both understanding and buying into the business goals. Employees are often the first voice customers or business partners hear. Any such initiatives should not only include getting employees informed about upcoming changes but also ensuring they fully understand and embrace what will happen and why. Only after employees have truly internalized the initiatives can they become the real drivers for the changes.

Finally, simplicity over complexity is vital for effective communication. Boomerang (a productivity software platform) conducted a study in 2016 based on over forty million emails to determine which factors led to responses. The results indicated that emails with 75–100 words had the highest response rate, at about 51 percent. The response rate decreased when emails were either too long or too short (Moore 2016).

Albert Einstein set the simplest rule for simplicity. "Everything should be made as simple as possible but not simpler." Achieving simplicity often takes sustained effort and leadership commitment. The natural human tendency is to have more. The challenge is always having the vigilance and clarity on what's truly essential. A business needs to make things simple for efficiency, competitiveness, and ultimate survival. Otherwise, you can collapse under the weight of your own complexity, like even the powerful Roman Empire.

If one hundred and fifty years ago, Ferdinand V. Hayden could navigate the complexity and uncertainties through effective communication to convince Congress to pass the Yellowstone Act, we should be able to use the tools and capabilities at our disposal for more efficient communication to achieve our business objectives. The challenge is how to find simplicity for effective communication in an increasingly complex world.

IMPLICATION

Technology advancements lead to efficient communication, but generally not effective communication, especially when it comes to cross-discipline or cross culture communications. For any business initiatives to be successful, leaders must cultivate a meaningful relationship that requires clear, honest, and reciprocal communication with the context of the issues being communicated.

LEADERSHIP EXERCISE

Look at your emails and tally how many times you used business jargons or acronyms that may be hard to understand. Also, track how many times you communicated in emails with people from different disciplines or different working cultures. Set a target and a reminder for yourself a month from now to reduce your use of jargon.

PART III

LEADERSHIP CASES

CHAPTER 12

YOU ARE A LEADER— NOW WHAT?

———

He who cannot be a good follower cannot be a good leader.

—*ARISTOTLE*

"... So can I just be honest with you, please? I'm not going to have a lot for you to do is the truth. And you being assigned to me is kind of just for me to set an example for the rest of the team. If you ask me, I think that you'd be much better off working in creative or marketing." What do you do when you have less than three minutes for an introduction with your new boss who has just told you that you were really not needed or wanted? That was a quote from the 2015 American comedy drama film *The Intern* by Nancy Meyers, a film starring Robert De Niro as Ben Whittaker, a seventy-year-old retiree who became a senior intern, and Anne Hathaway as Jules Owston, the CEO of a fast-growing e-commerce fashion start-up *About The Fit*.

During the seventeen years of my career with ExxonMobil, I had twelve different managers and eight different roles in various businesses. Every job is different, and every manager has different expectation or preferred way of engagement. With the dynamically changing business environment and the rapid adoption of new technologies, the trend of frequent job changes is likely going to continue, regardless of whether between companies or within the same company. In the technology industry, the pace of turnover is even faster than in traditional industries. According to a CNBC report, the medium tenure on Google's teams is 1.1 years (Bean 2019). As an aspiring leader, it is likely you will be facing situations of becoming a leader on a new team, sometimes even unexpectedly, without fully knowing your responsibility.

Ben Whittaker in the movie had many years of leadership experience in a completely different industry, printing phone books. As an "intern" now, Ben obviously does not have much authority. However, it does not mean he cannot be an effective leader. The story is theatrical, but the scenario is not that different from many who become new leaders.

There are some very interesting and comical scenes that show how Ben slowly wins over coworkers with his thoughtful leadership, gains Jules's respect and appreciation, and eventually becomes a trusted friend, adviser and mentor for Jules.

If you have just entered a new role, you may be excited about the leadership opportunities. Yet excitement may or may not always be the emotion for everyone around you. You may be anxious about all the things you have to learn very quickly, but eager to show the world your skills and expertise. At the same time, the people you are going to be working with all likely have some pre-conceived notions of who you are and what you should be doing in your new role.

In their book, *You Are in Charge—Now What,* Neff and Citrin (2005) described that many seeds of destructions for new leaders are sown in the first hundred days. Although the book was more geared toward senior executives, the advice is relevant to everyone who just became a new leader or moved to a new role. No matter what your profession is and what level you are at, you can expect to experience many career or job transitions, either between companies or within the same company.

Leadership principles apply everywhere, but there are some unique challenges for new leaders in establishing credibility and setting expectations. As a new leader, you often need to "learn how to fly on the way down." The biggest myth about leaders is that they know the answers. In reality, new leaders need to think big since thinking big is the only way to know the potentials for you and your organization. At the same time, you have to act humble and human.

ESTABLISH TRUST THROUGH ALIGNMENT OF EXPECTATIONS

One should appreciate that different organizations have different ways of doing things and different people have very different expectations. I have had managers who sent emails at two o'clock in the morning and expected replies first thing in the morning. I also had bosses who much preferred to knock on my office door rather than send an email. Some expect regular updates, while others let you run completely on your own. And while email is the universal means for business communication in the United States, WeChat is the primary medium for businesspeople in China.

In the movie, while Ben's expectation is to have the excitement "to have a place to go, feel needed and even challenged," Jules was simply nudged to fulfill a company obligation, a community outreach program for "senior interns." She had no expectations for any meaningful contribution from the role. Since Jules is under pressure to cope with the workload, having grown her company from a start-up founded in her kitchen to a two hundred twenty employee juggernaut, she did not want the intern to take up her precious time.

At the end of the somewhat awkward introduction, Ben made sure he understood Jules's expectation for the rules of engagement, while Jules clearly did not want to give him any real work by saying, "I will email you when I have something for you to do."

"Or I can just stop by a few times a day to check in." Ben politely tested her.

"I will email you," Jules replied sternly.

At the end of the conversation, Ben restated what Jules said "I will wait to hear from you... I look forward to it."

It is a minor exchange but illustrates how important it is to ensure alignment of expectations. Any time you are in a new role, there are opportunities for misaligned expectations. More importantly, it is essential to proactively calibrate expectations from your stakeholders for your new role. Do not assume what's on the job description is really your job and do not assume what you were told before you got the role is still the same.

Very often, even managers may not know what the job really is. You have to figure out or define your own job. When that happens, you can either get frustrated or take it as a perfect opportunity to demonstrate your leadership.

ESTABLISH CREDIBILITY BASED ON BUILDING TRUST AND EXPERTISE

In Chapter 7, we talked about Mr. Richard Roca, the newly appointed director of the Applied Physics Laboratory. He spent the first three months on the job simply listening. He met his sponsors, program managers, lab management, staff, and potential business partners in the community. Only then did he start to work with his leadership team to define that "success for APL meant making critical contributions to critical sponsor challenges."

In one of the scenes in the movie, when Ben is driving Jules to the company warehouse, Jules questions the route Ben is going to take on the way to the company warehouse.

"No, no. Make a right. Ninth to Hamilton to the expressway," Jules said.

"I think we should take Fourth to Flatbush. Much faster," replied Ben.

"It won't be," Jules said, somewhat annoyed.

"By twelve minutes. At least," Ben said.

Ben does not specifically tell Jules that she is wrong. Instead, he asks Jules again, "Can I try?"

When they arrive at the warehouse, Jules realizes Ben is right and offers an apology to Ben.

When you are in a new position, it is important to recognize that you have to be confident when you need to be and humble when you are not sure in order to establish trust and credibility. Avoid conflict without purpose, but earn the right to be assertive and constructive by being authentic and honest. You earn the trust through being competent and transparent consistently. Conversely, know what your boundaries are where you must speak up; for example, in the film, Ben held a firm stand when he saw Jules's driver drinking, clearly unacceptable behavior in any organization.

INSPIRE PEOPLE BY KNOWING WHAT MOTIVATES THEM

In the fast-paced world we are in, we tend to focus on efficient ways of communication by email, texting, or instant messaging. The reality is none of those tools contain any information about the writer's underlying emotions. Neither do they have any body language to decipher. When it comes to connecting with people, there is no replacement for face-to-face time when you can look into their eyes directly.

As a newcomer who stands out easily in the company, Ben would not only spend time to get to know the people by providing a helping hand when needed, but also making an effort to understand their underlying issues and concerns in order to better connect with them as individuals.

Many new leaders don't understand what truly motivates their team and its members. They often assume that what motivates others is the same as what motivates themselves. Another common misconception is that 'money' is the key motivating factor when that's rarely the case. Although monetary reward is important, it's unlikely that it will be the only thing that employees find motivating.

Some people may be motivated by flexible working arrangements as they are seeking a greater work/life balance. Others will be motivated by factors such as achievement and extra responsibility. Some might love the opportunity for travel while others might be motivated by the alignment of the company's purpose with societal issues. The key is to find out what motivates each person on the team and work to provide it.

MENTORING CAN GO BOTH WAYS

Traditional mentorship involves a more senior person, advising junior or younger person for their development. The concept of reverse mentoring is gaining more acceptance in some organizations. In reverse mentoring, the senior leader is mentored by a younger or more junior employee. The process recognizes that there are skills gaps and opportunities to learn on both sides of a mentoring relationship. Reverse mentoring can be an effective approach for specific skills (e.g., digital capabilities, understanding specific cultural contexts to do business in a different part of the world) or more broad organizational culture driven needs (e.g., diversity and inclusion initiatives, retention of the younger workforce). A 2017 Huffington report on the reserve mentoring program at Pershing, a BNY Mellon Company, cited a set of powerful statistics that showed a 96 percent retention rate of its seventy-seven participants who had rotated through the reverse mentoring program between 2013 to 2016 (Kantor 2017).

While waiting for the introduction meeting with Jules, Ben took the opportunity to ask her assistant, Becky, for advice.

"Any tips before we go in?" Ben asked.

"Just talk fast. She hates slow talkers. [...] Don't dawdle in any way. Just keep it moving and don't forget to blink. Blink. Yeah, she hates when people don't blink. It weirds her out. [...] There you go. Go, go. Go."

Sure enough, you would notice that Ben blinked a few times in the movie.

At the same time, Ben was ready to offer his advice to Jules when the opportunity arises.

Jules is under pressure to give up her post as CEO to someone outside the company, as her investors feel she is unable to cope with the workload.

Ben greatly encourages Jules to think about how much this will change her authority and how her creativity may be hindered. More importantly, he reminds her of her passion for her company that cannot be replicated.

"You remember the day I drove you to the warehouse? [...] Okay, well I stood in the back, and I watched you show the workers how to fold and box the clothes. [...] No one else is ever going to have that kind of commitment to your company, Jules. To me, it's pretty simple. *About The Fit* needs you and, if you don't mind me saying, you need it. Someone may come in with more experience than you but they're never going to know what you know."

"It is in a moment like this when you need someone you know you can count on," Jules acknowledged.

On the one hand, new leaders need to be humble and show a willingness to listen and learn. On the other hand, new leaders can also bring fresh perspectives to a new organization. When it comes to mentoring, it can go both ways.

Regardless of which side of the mentoring relationship you are in, a healthy mentoring relationship can become an effective conduit for better connecting an organization's objectives with personal leadership values.

HELP YOURSELF BY HELPING OTHERS TO SUCCEED

While the business world is a very competitive place, we achieve our success by helping others achieve their dreams. At the same time, we also find the purpose and values for our life aligned with our leadership value.

"I have a business degree, but I never seem to do anything right around here. [...] I bust my ass for her fourteen hours a day and she never notices." Becky, the twenty-four-year-old Wharton graduate working as the assistant for Jules, was overwhelmed by the constant demands and frustrated by the fact Jules was not recognizing the amount of work she was doing.

Becky was naturally surprised and felt slighted when she was told the seventy-year-old intern Ben was going to help her.

Ben quickly came up with some business insights about customer spending patterns, but more importantly, he made sure to let Jules know Becky's contribution. He did not stop there. He reminded Jules about Becky's qualifications and also nudged Jules to commit to personally acknowledge Becky's workload.

In summary, leadership is a choice. Leaders take action, empower, and inspire the people around them. Leaders make the people around them better. The best way to succeed as a new leader is to help others succeed.

Would you consider Ben a leader?

IMPLICATION

New leaders often get to their positions because they have great expertise. However, the talents that make a person successful in a previous individual contributor role are rarely the same ones that will make them excel as leaders. Many new leaders are ambitious and tend to adopt a 'commander'-like mindset in which they micromanage, telling direct reports exactly what to do and when to do it. In contrast, humble leaders are more driven to learn and improve in a new environment. Humility doesn't weaken leaders' authority. It gives them more flexibility in how they use their power.

LEADERSHIP EXERCISE

If you are a new leader, take proactive steps to figure out who are your key stakeholders and ensure your expectations are aligned with those of your stakeholders. Develop a ninety-day plan with thirty-day and sixty-day milestones along the way to define your priorities and enhance your chances of success.

CHAPTER 13

CAREER CHANGE CAN BE AN OPPORTUNITY FOR IMPACT

In times of change, learners will inherit the earth while the learned will find themselves beautifully equipped to deal with a world that no longer exists.

—ERIC HOFFER

I have engaged with probably hundreds of start-up companies over my career, but one 2021 meeting that stands out as distinctively different was with Jeremy Suard, CEO of Exodigo, a start-up company based in Israel that developed a technology for underground detection for construction projects. Instead of presenting technology or capabilities, he spent the first thirty minutes of the meeting asking questions: testing and validating assumptions about the industry, about how we manage construction projects, the relationship between us as the owner vs. contractors, the risks and unknowns. Only at the end of the meeting did he very briefly describe the development stage of the start-up's technology and its capabilities.

I reached out to Jeremy when I was writing the book and asked him about his approach. He shared with me that he was with the Israeli special operations forces before he ventured into entrepreneurship.

"When you are in special operations force, you cannot afford to assume anything." He explained to me how they had to validate every single detail before going out for a mission. It was often a life and death situation.

He brought that mindset from his military experience to his business approach and applied that perfectly. For a start-up, validating assumptions is critical to success, yet it is often an overlooked activity by many start-up companies. In fact, when I, as an industry mentor, was mentoring another start-up, Osmoses, through the National Science Foundation I-Corp program, I was pleasantly surprised to learn the entire thrust of the program focused on validating assumptions about customers or markets.

EMPLOYEE TENURES ARE GETTING SHORTER

Companies used to hire, develop, and expect employees to work long careers for the company. In fact, several of my colleagues on my team retired with forty years of dedicated service in the same company. However, the world is changing and changing fast. According to the US Bureau of Labor Statistics, the median number of years that wage and salary workers had with their current employers was 4.1 years. Furthermore, the median tenure for workers ages 25–34 is 2.8 years.

While longevity can be rewarded with a pension and other benefits, staying too long with one company can also give the impression that you are not interested in growing your career. Even within the same company, people often move between different functions or sometimes completely different roles due to either personal interests or organizational needs. From a macro-level, even the average life span of companies in the S&P 500 has been declining, falling from about ninety years in 1935 to the current about seventeen years (Handscomb and Thaker 2018, Hillenbrand et al. 2019). Those changes often force employees to seek alternative career options.

What does this mean for leadership development? How do we carry leadership from one job to another? What aspects of your leadership stay the same and what aspects of your leadership have to change and adapt? It is always better to have a mental framework to guide the changes rather than being reactive to specific circumstances when things occur.

Tim Lynch, partner at McChrystal Group, explained to me his perspective. "For me, part of leadership is trying to understand intellectually, both on a cognitive and emotional level, what the situation requires me to become in order to affect the outcome that I want to achieve? What characteristics do I display? Is it strength or humility, is it confidence or vulnerability? How do I interact with my external environment or the atmospherics?"

TRANSITION FROM TECHNICAL TO BUSINESS

Transitioning from a technical role to a business role is a common career path for many in the industrial working environment where moving to business management is often, rightly or wrongly, viewed as a more exciting career path. It is important to point out the differences in the nature of technical problem-solving and business management. Fundamentally, business management focuses on business objectives and generally has the desired outcome formulated from the start, while engineers and scientists with a problem-solving and exploratory mindset tend to shift focus depending on where the new information or facts lead to.

In a broader sense, the same mindset also applies to the discussion about specialists vs. generalists. The following is what Bill Gates wrote in one of his Gates Notes about the book, *Range: Why Generalists Triumph in a Specialized World,* by the *New York Times* bestselling author David Epstein (2019). "I believe that one of the key reasons Microsoft took off is because we thought more broadly than other startups of that era. We hired not just brilliant coders but people who had real breadth within their field and across domains. I discovered that these team members are the most curious and had the deepest mental models."

- While people with a technical background enjoy the advantage of their analytical skills in dealing with business issues, they, at the same time, must recognize the differences in mindsets for dealing with business issues in order to be successful in the transition.
- While technical problems tend to have a unique answer, which is the right answer, business issues in the real-world

rarely have one unique solution. It is often a fruitless exercise to find the right or best answer. Making a wrong decision is, in most cases, better than making no decision at all. The frequent lack of any "right" answer, can be foreign territory to technical people.

- Technically trained people tend to view the world as a complicated but deterministic machine. As discussed in Chapter 8, there is a fundamental difference between complicated problems vs. complex problems. While a technical or analytical approach works well for complicated problems, solving complex problems often requires a different approach by focusing on actions, or learning by doing.

- Technically trained people naturally tend to focus on technical solutions. In the real-world, business solutions can often be a more effective alternative. For example, it is often cheaper to seek out a license for a patent than trying to design around a patent. It is important to be able to overcome the inherent bias and stay open to new approaches.

- Perfection is the enemy of good enough. Technical people, including myself, strive for perfection, and oftentimes, rightfully so, we want to show the best efforts we can to solve a problem. However, we need to always balance the organizational needs versus our desire for perfection and always calibrate the effort against the expected return.

- While unique and creative ideas are often positively recognized and encouraged in the technical field, you will more likely be challenged in the business world for doing things outside of the norm. Creativity is important for innovation regardless of your role. However, it is important to take the time to understand why things are done in a certain way first.

In summary, people with deep specialized knowledge could often benefit from a mindset that avoids one single approach or unique solution on business issues. Be open-minded and develop the ability to connect dots from different perspectives can often lead to better decisions and better results.

TRANSITION BETWEEN BUSINESS ENVIRONMENTS

Twenty years ago, I flew from the US to Jakarta for a business meeting with a senior executive from one of the largest national companies in Indonesia. The company was an important customer, and we considered the meeting important. A few hours before the meeting, my local contact reached out to the office of the executive to ensure he was ready for the meeting. To our surprise, he had completely forgotten about the meeting and was in a car repair shop getting work done on his car. He offered to meet us in the shop for a discussion if we could make it there in time.

We decided to take up the offer and drove to the shop on a crowded, narrow street. The meeting was obviously casual, but the discussion went well. We accomplished our business objective, in an unusual setting, but got a better sense of his business needs for our decision-making.

If you are working in different parts of the world, you have to learn to adapt not only to the working culture, but also to the macro business environments.

Many global companies have large footprints in both the US and China, the world's two largest economies. However, the business environments are quite different. While the US is mostly a market-driven economy where business dynamics are mostly driven by the invisible hand, Chinese government policy plays a much more visible role in driving macroeconomic developments. While my experience speaks to specific differences between two critical but very different markets, it highlights the unique type of challenges associated with transitioning between environments shaped by different forces and mindsets.

The development and execution of a business strategy is a core activity for any business and most Western businesses have a structured process for developing their strategy. A strategy provides a north star to follow through the noise of daily business and a changing environment. There are many different approaches to strategy development, but most involve analyzing a market's supply and demand balance and the competitive positioning needed to take advantage of the firm's competitive advantage. For established firms, they often rely on historical information or industrial studies to project future opportunities.

There is a fundamental difference when it comes to analyzing opportunities and risks in the Chinese market: the impact of government policy. On the one hand, the Chinese government decades ago dismantled key elements of central planning (such as price controls and production quotas) and drastically reduced state ownership in the economy. On the other hand, the government still has a five-year economic planning process which, to a large extent, sets economic priorities for the coming five years. While most Western companies have sophisticated capabilities for market analyses, few companies traditionally have a structured approach to include the intricate Chinese policymaking dynamic in their business decision processes.

The reality is the need to work cooperatively with government agencies and bureaucrats is perhaps greater in China than in any other country in the world. Even in countries where the shadow is not as pervasive, companies need to have a better understanding of those different dynamics rather than making assumptions.

Some companies, especially European companies, do it well by having the right people who understand China's market, know its business environment, are culturally savvy, and have sufficient credibility in the organization to influence business decisions. But it is still a challenge to incorporate Chinese government policymaking dynamics into the formal corporate decision-making process in a structured way. Many companies stumble and learn by making mistakes.

Without debating the quality and merits of those government policies, it is important for businesses to not just appreciate the impact of the policies, but more importantly the intent of those policies. I have seen increased transparency in government communications on policies, but it takes more effort to understand the underlying intent of those policies. It is often companies with those insights that can better leverage government support to progress their interests.

As an aspiring leader, working between different business environments can be both exciting and challenging. An effective leader can better communicate and articulate not only how things are done differently, but more importantly why things are done differently so organizations can have the context to make more informed decisions.

TRANSITION BETWEEN MILITARY TO CIVILIAN

According to the US Department of Labor, there were 158 million civilians in the total labor force, and of those, 8.9 million were veterans. Veterans represent 5.6 percent of the total civilian labor force in the United States (Hylton 2021). All branches of the military have a heavy focus on leadership, partly because of the frequent need for new leaders created by the high turnover rate. With that said, military leadership is not always the same as what is needed to succeed in a corporate setting. The transition can be challenging for some veterans.

I am far from qualified to discuss military leadership since I never had any direct military experience myself. However, a few common themes emerge during my conversations with several military veterans who had successfully transitioned to civilian leadership roles.

First of all, military actions are often mission driven. Because of this focus on the mission, there's often a more clearly defined objective in the military. Mission drives purpose. Mission drives connection. Mission drives camaraderie. Many of those skills gained in the military setting can be valuable in the business world, as illustrated in the example of Jeremy Suard at the beginning of the chapter.

"The Marine Corps is very specific on the sequence in order of importance. And inside the Marine Corps, mission accomplishment is the priority. Your welfare is second to the priority, or second to mission accomplishment." Tim Lynch, partner at McChrystal Group, explained to me that did not mean you would neglect your marines. It is actually the opposite. You really need to take care of your marines to make sure they can accomplish the mission. "But when it comes down to do I get a few extra hours of sleep, or do I hit my objective, sleep goes away."

In contrast, purpose and objective for business activities are not always as defined. In fact, creating clarity is an area organizations and teams often struggle with. Leadership is about creating clarity from the chaos, from uncertainties. In addition, mission inside a business is not the only center people live their life in order to achieve work life balance.

Second, the military generally has a more clearly defined command-and-control organizational structure vs. matrix organizations often seen in the civilian world. The balance between leading and influencing can be somewhat different. A friend of mine told me an interesting anecdote observation after she transferred from a civilian hospital to VA hospital. She observed very different behavior between the patients. Her patients in the VA hospital, mostly veterans, were more likely to follow doctor's instructions than her civilian patients. For someone transitioning from a military role to a civilian role, it would likely take a different mindset to lead.

With those differences, there are many unique leadership qualities that veterans possess that they could leverage to be successful in making the most of the experience gained when they serve the country. Adaptability, taking initiative, and critical thinking are among some of the more important skills. Most importantly, everyone in the military is taught to do the right thing, even when no one is looking. The value of integrity is a fundamental asset to any organization.

Consistent with what we discussed in Chapter 3, veterans could benefit by consciously developing a list of unique values and skill sets gained through military service and think about how they can leverage those unique strengths in any new organizations and new careers they want to pursue.

In a broader context, a similar principle can be applied for people who gained experience from a highly structured work environment, be it military, corporate, or the government as they transition into a less structured environment like a start-up or non-profit.

In summary, leadership is contextual. Effective leadership changes from situation to situation. To be most effective and successful, effective leaders stay grounded in ethical values but use a growth and learning mindset. They are fixed and flexible at the same time, never straying from ethics but always willing to adapt to the circumstances. More importantly, they have an open mind and are willing to learn. People with the right mindset are likely to have a better chance to formally or informally access and synthesize new information, whether it means connecting their current task with something they had experience with or developing a new mental framework for making the right decisions. The approach by Jeremy Suard of Exodigo was a good example.

IMPLICATION

During transitions between different roles, especially between organizations with different cultures, it is always important to appreciate the context of the leadership needed for the new organization and how you may need to make decisions differently. At a personal level, it is also important to have clarity in how to carry your leadership forward, knowing what aspects of your leadership should stay the same and what aspects should change and adapt.

LEADERSHIP EXERCISE

Identify the last time you transitioned from one organization to another and use it as an example to reflect on the surprises and learnings in terms of what aspects of your leadership you had to change and adapt. As an alternative, develop a hypothetical scenario about a role you would like to seek, and develop a detailed plan on what aspects of leadership behavior you need to change for the new role and how you would manage those changes.

CHAPTER 14

CHANGE STARTS
WITH RIPPLES

———

The greatest danger in times of turbulence is not the turbulence—it is to act with yesterday's logic.

—PETER DRUCKER

I was watching TV in 2017 when Rex Tillerson, who just became the secretary of state, was getting off a government plane for the first time. Many at ExxonMobil, where Rex was the CEO for ten years, noted he was the only person holding the handrail when the group was getting off the plane. The leadership challenges he faced in driving changes in the US State Department and his ability or inability to influence then President Trump are widely reported but beyond my capacity to write. However, I want to write about this handrail observation most people likely missed.

Safety is a fundamental part of the business culture at ExxonMobil. Holding the handrail while walking on the stairs is a requirement which becomes second nature for everyone who works for the company. And the CEO is no exception.

Every organization has written as well as unwritten rules defining how the organization should function. More importantly, every organization has established practices that have served the business well at some point of time. At the same time, leaders often must challenge the status quo and change the order of things for the better. Leaders make progress.

According to a recent book by Beau Breslin, *A Constitution for The Living: Imagining How Five Generations of Americans Would Rewrite the Nation's Fundamental Law,* Thomas Jefferson thought every generation should change the nation's fundamental law. "The earth belongs... to the living, the dead have neither powers nor rights over it." So proclaimed Thomas Jefferson. The United States instead, by and large, followed the counsel of James Madison, who argued the nation's longevity would be best secured by a constitution which endures over many generations in order to keep the nation strong and united (Breslin 2021).

Among all the challenges leaders face, leading change is among the most difficult. Changing the direction of a large organization is always hard, but even small changes in business practices can be very difficult to implement without having a thoughtful approach. The most important time to set into place a positive vision is during a time of confusion when everyone is looking for answers. As is the case we discussed in Chapter 7 when Andy Grove and Gordon Moore made the monumental decision of getting Intel out of the memory business and focusing on the microprocessor business.

At a broader level, today's world energy trilemma—security, affordability, and sustainability—is creating challenges or opportunities for many companies to reassess their business priorities.

When changes are prompted by external factors such as natural disasters or the current pandemic, the debate is less about whether to change, but about what and how to change in order to effectively deal with the challenges. The current discussion about the future of work prompted or accelerated by the pandemic is an example for many organizations. However, when one tries to create change without obvious near-term organization urgency created by external conditions, the inertia for most people or organization is to stay with the status quo. As humans, we are hardwired to resist changes unless we have to change.

While working at Arthur D. Little in the early sixties, David Gleicher created a formula, later refined by Kathie Dannemiller, for change on three things (Dannemiller and Jacobs 1992):
- Dissatisfaction with the status quo
- A vision for the future
- First concrete steps to make the vision a reality

Organizations tend to remain static unless there is a force greater than the inertia of the status quo that keeps us chained to the past. The product of these three forces has to be greater than the resistance in the organization in order to for change to happen. How can we apply this framework to drive organizational change?

DISSATISFACTION WITH THE STATUS QUO

As an amateur photographer, I watch developments in the photography industry more closely than most people. The biggest news in the industry in the year 2022 is that both Nikon and Canon, the two most recognized brands, are halting development of new SLR cameras and are shifting their focus to mirrorless cameras.

SLR cameras use a mirror and prism system that permits the photographer to look through the lens and see exactly what will be captured. Mirrorless cameras, on the other hand, eliminate the reflex mirror, and thus make the camera much more compact and lighter without compromising quality.

Until about five years ago, almost all professional photographers used SLR cameras, but today only about 36 percent of them use SLRs while 63 percent have transitioned to mirrorless cameras (Condon 2022). This is a seismic change. The photography business, a $20 billion global market, has been a very brutal business that is continuously being recreated by disruptive innovation.

For many decades, the industry had gone through the same steady and predictable growth as many other industries until early this century. However, few industries have gone through the complete rebirth that the photography industry has due to disruptive technologies.

The good news is that photography is getting more popular than ever before. The bad news is that photography's growing popularity is being driven by smartphones. Shipments of smartphones with built-in cameras surpassed 1.57 billion in 2020, twelve times higher than the peak of digital cameras sold (121 million in 2010). And as of 2020, only 8.89 million digital cameras were sold, with only 2.93 million of those being mirrorless cameras. This means about 0.57 percent of consumer cameras were sold as dedicated cameras, and only 0.2 percent were the newest innovation: mirrorless cameras.

If we can borrow the Arthur D. Little framework for change discussed earlier, how would a traditional camera company articulate the "dissatisfaction?" Until recently, SLR cameras were regarded as a better option than mirrorless for action photography due to their speed. Like many organizations, dissatisfaction associated with the status quo, or SLR cameras in this case, is not always apparent unless they are compared against something. Mirrorless cameras in the last few years have quickly caught up or surpassed SLR performance by adopting new technical approaches.

As a result, both Nikon and Canon are now, somewhat belatedly, shifting their efforts to mirrorless cameras. However, I wonder if the change is coming too late and they are solving a problem of yesterday.

Sources of dissatisfaction can come from a variety of external or internal sources. Leaving that dissatisfaction to fester can lead to lagging behind other better-performing organizations, or in the worst-case, can even be a matter of survival. In the case of cameras, the cycle for disruptive innovation is getting shorter and often from outside the core businesses. It is getting increasingly difficult to anticipate who will be competitors in a dynamic world. The rapid adoption of smartphones and emergence of drone camera are examples which have fundamentally changed the camera industry.

Leaders need to have a healthy perspective of the external market, rather than just the internal organization, in order to spot inflection points early when disruptive forces arrive.

A VISION FOR THE FUTURE

When Malala Yousafzai was shot in the face for speaking out for girls' education in Pakistan, she could have made the decision that this was not something she could change. Instead, she chose to continue the fight until every girl could go to school. And on the way, she became the youngest ever Nobel Laureate in December 2014 at the age of seventeen.

One-hundred years ago, on March 4, 1917, Jeannette Rankin became the first woman to serve in the US Congress, representing Montana. Rankin's election was extraordinary, as it happened about three years before US women had the right to vote. She actively worked on women's voting rights as a student volunteer in Washington state. She later became the first woman to address the Montana legislature when she testified in support of women's suffrage. She could have accepted the fact that she was not even eligible to vote at the time, but Rankin instead took advantage of the fact that there were no laws forbidding women from holding federal office.

In 1967, Kathrine Switzer became the first woman to officially run a marathon when she completed the Boston Marathon before women were allowed to compete. She was not deterred by the fact that there was no women's running team anywhere at the time. She trained with the men's cross-country team instead. When her coach told her the marathon was too long a distance for her, she convinced him to run thirty-one miles with her three weeks before the fateful Boston Marathon. During her Boston run on April 19, a race official attempted to stop Switzer until he was shoved to the ground by Switzer's boyfriend. She not only completed the race but also became the women's winner of the 1974 New York City Marathon.

In a business context, creating a different vision for the future often requires strategic change and rallying the organization behind the vision. The example we discussed in Chapter 6 described how VW announced its new vision, phasing out internal combustion engine vehicles. Herbert Diess, CEO of VW, galvanized his organization by inviting his main competitor, Tesla CEO Elon Musk, to call in to an internal conference with two hundred VW top executives (Dow 2021).

A vision for change can be as grand as those of Yousafzai, Rankin or Diess, but can also be more personal or oriented for a small working team. Within a team or smaller organization, it is much easier to drive change by leveraging aligned organizational strategy, rather than simply by power or authority. The key is to have organizational buy-in for the new vision and justification for change.

As an example, in the current business environment where investors are increasingly scrutinizing companies on ESG, leaders have to galvanize their organization in order to drive real change, rather than simply making changes to meet regulatory requirements. Leaders have to not only establish necessary processes for new business practices but also clearly articulate ESG as a fundamental responsibility to stakeholders.

FIRST CONCRETE STEPS TO MAKE THE VISION A REALITY

You have probably seen people arrange all kinds of domino chains with tens of thousands of domino pieces falling in sequence. Most domino exhibitions feature tiles that are all the same size.

In a slightly different variation, J. M. J. van Leeuwen, a physicist at Leiden University in the Netherlands, using a mathematical model, predicted a domino can knock over, at the maximum, a subsequent domino twice its size. He recorded a YouTube video which illustrates the effect with thirteen dominos, where each one is about one and a half times larger than the previous one. The smallest domino, a mere 5 mm tall, eventually leads to the downfall of a 1m tall domino. According to the video, the final domino would have grown to the size of the Empire State Building if he had placed twenty-nine dominos (Morris 2009).

As individuals, we often feel like the most insignificant thread in the tapestry of life. A false sense of humility can prevent us from seeing that everyone on this planet has been equipped with the potential for making a meaningful difference, either in an organization or society.

Mother Teresa once said, "I alone cannot change the world, but I can cast a stone across the water to create many ripples." For Mother Teresa, those ripples included over 4500 nuns active in 133 countries, managing homes for people suffering from HIV/AIDS, leprosy, and tuberculosis. The congregation also runs soup kitchens, dispensaries, mobile clinics, children's and family counseling programs, as well as orphanages and schools.

In order for change to take root, it is not sufficient just to have a vision for the changed world, but also to know where to start the change process. Understand what you can change independently without triggering pushback and have a credible roadmap on the changes necessary for the larger change to take hold.

I dreamed about running a marathon when I was young, but never thought it would be possible due to the tremendous commitment and discipline needed for training. That dream sat in the back of my mind until some twenty-five years later, when I finally had the courage to sign up for and actually finish my first marathon in 2009.

As I reflect on my marathon journey, I realize it also followed a similar pattern. About fifteen years ago, I realized I was not able to continue playing basketball both due to the need for a committed schedule with others, and the rigor required for contact sports. There was a dissatisfaction in the status quo. That dream of running a marathon that had sat in the back of my mind slowly started coming back. I started some regular running, but my job at the time required frequent international travel, which always disrupted my training schedule. To keep up my routine, I began packing a pair of running shoes when I traveled. I took the opportunity to run not only on the streets of Beijing, Seoul, Tokyo, Dubai, Shanghai, Moscow and London, but also along the Copacabana beach and the Danube River. In addition, I developed a habit of hitting the gym in the wee hours of the morning for a tempo run to help adjust to jet lag.

After building a routine and training regularly, I finally had the courage to sign up for my first marathon. I set a goal for myself that I wanted to qualify for the Boston Marathon. Fourteen years later, I still have not been able to qualify for the Boston Marathon. However, I am proud of the fact that I have completed thirteen marathons, including one I ran alone during the pandemic in 2020.

Driving change at a personal level is hard, and it certainly can be even more challenging to make change in a large organization or at the societal level. However, with the right idea, thoughtful planning, and the right organizational support, a small ripple can gain momentum, create a cascade of changes, and eventually lead to an unstoppable wave for transformation.

On the evening of September 4, 1920, Liu Bannong, a Chinese student sitting in a London flat, wrote a short poem, not knowing it would become one of the most popular Chinese poems of the century (Liu 1920). A sequence of four short stanzas of identical format bearing the title "How Could I Not Miss Her." The poem was written as a reflection of his longing for his motherland, rather than a faraway lover.

The poem itself is very sentimental and poetic, but more significantly, Liu invented a new Chinese character in the poem for "She", or "Her" in the English context (Chinese uses the same character for "She" and "Her"). During the time in London as a linguistic student, he was involved in translating Western literature into Chinese. It was then he often encountered the difficulties in translating English "she" to Chinese since Chinese at the time had only a word equivalent to "he." He often had to refer "she" as "the other female" or "female he" which were obviously awkward. It is interesting to note that the equivalent expression in Japanese today still uses 彼 (かれ) for male and 彼女 (かのじょ) for female by adding the word female to the word for "he", though it is more customary to use their name, or social or family role, rather than a third person pronoun.

When Liu was writing the poem, he decided to create a new character for "she" (她) which was similar to the Chinese character for "he" (他), but he replaced the left side of the character with a radical which literally means female (女). In retrospect, it is a brilliant creation, but at the time was very controversial. Not only the conservatives in China at the time attacked Liu for his creation, even some females who were advocating for gender equality questioned the wisdom of separating the word by gender. Today, the character "She" (她) is used mostly for a third person female, but also symbolically for motherland.

It was a small step, but his willingness to break the status quo, an important trait for leaders, led to a profound change in a language which has been around for thousands of years.

The business world is getting increasingly complex and interconnected, and so are most organizations. One of the challenges for many who strive to effect change is how to navigate the intricate cobweb in interconnected and interlinked organizations. Changing one thing could trigger many other changes the organization may not be ready to deal with yet.

As an example, digital transformation is a buzz word used in every organization in the past few years. Yet a widely cited study by McKinsey showed that success rate is only at 26 percent even for digitally savvy industries. For traditional companies, the success rate is at a dismal range of about 4–11 percent (Boutetiere et al. 2018). Many initiatives fail because the transformation focuses on technology, rather than the underlying process of organizational culture change.

In summary, if you want to drive organizational change, either transformational or incremental, you need to develop a clear case for action based on the pain of the current state, paint a picture of what the future would look like so others can see, and take small concrete steps to show the organization change is possible.

Mahatma Gandhi said it well, "In a gentle way, you can shake the world."

IMPLICATION

Organizations tend to remain static unless there is a force greater than the inertia of the status quo. Contrary to common perception, people are not afraid of change. Instead, people are afraid of uncertainties. One needs to have a thoughtful framework in order for the change to take roots. Ability to articulate the dissatisfaction to the status quo and paint a vision for the future are important, but identification of a first concrete small step for implementation is often critical to make the vision into reality.

LEADERSHIP EXERCISE

Identify one practice in your organization that you would like to change and use Arthur D. Little framework to define the dissatisfaction associated with the status quo, paint a picture for the future, and identify the first concrete step for change.

CHAPTER 15

THE CORPORATE LADDER IS TOO CROWDED

The most difficult thing is the decision to act, the rest is merely tenacity.

—*AMELIA EARHART*

"Leadership is something you earn, something you're chosen for. You can't come in yelling, 'I'm your leader!' If it happens, it's because the other guys respect you." That's a quote from Ben Roethlisberger, the retired Pittsburgh Steelers quarterback in the NFL who became the youngest Super Bowl winning quarterback in NFL history by leading the Steelers in Super Bowl XL at the age of twenty-three. Roethlisberger got his chance to play as the third quarterback on the team the previous season due to injuries to the two veteran quarterbacks ahead of him. In the 2005 season Super Bowl game against the Seattle Seahawks, Roethlisberger did not play his best in the big game. In fact, he had one of the worst passing games of his career. But he did what was necessary to win the game. Similarly, Tom Brady, as a second-year backup, demonstrated his unflappable skills after Drew Bledsoe, the starting quarterback, was injured. The Patriots, led by Tom Brady, went on an amazing run of nine Super Bowl appearances, resulting in six championships in the subsequent two decades.

Both Ben Roethlisberger and Tom Brady obviously had the skills, but more importantly they took full advantage of the unexpected opportunities bestowed upon them by being ready. This is beautifully articulated by Winston Churchill, "To each, there comes in their lifetime a special moment when they are figuratively tapped on the shoulder and offered the chance to do a very special thing…what a tragedy if that moment finds them unprepared for that which could have been their finest hour."

All organizations invest tremendous resources to establish the confidence for aspiring leaders to take on new responsibilities and grow into leaders. However, the world is becoming increasingly dynamic and unpredictable. The traditional business approach of strategy, planning, and execution is increasingly being challenged. As a result, leaders are required to be adaptive, agile, and nimble to cope with the seismic shifts. The traditional defined career path may not work anymore. Aspiring leaders today must remain nimble since navigating the unexpected is increasingly becoming the new normal.

BE READY WHEN OPPORTUNITY KNOCKS

Unfortunately, there are two different challenges to "being prepared."

First of all, it is not always obvious what to prepare for. There is often no warning about our next position in the same organization or the next job. As we discussed in Chapter 13, the median tenure for workers ages 25–34 is about 2.8 years. Instead of preparing for a specific job, aspiring leaders need to crystallize what it takes to maximize their potential, and what leadership means at a personal level. Those reflections can guide you to seek out and prepare for opportunities which are more aligned with your personal values and purpose.

The second challenge is the so-called "permission paradox" which was described in the book *The Five Patterns of Extraordinary Careers* almost twenty years ago (Citrin and Smith 2005). "You cannot get the experience without the job, yet you cannot get the job without the experience." The "permission paradox" is a challenge facing many during their careers and can be a paralyzing obstacle to overcome for many aspiring leaders. The authors described some tactics in order to get out of the paradox by turning implied permission into direct permission and turning permission into action.

The authors also pointed out that, based on extensive work they did at Spencer Stuart, there is a limited number of life-changing opportunities in people's working career. If taken full advantage of, those opportunities will positively and dramatically change people's career direction, as are the examples of Ben Roethlisberger and Tom Brady.

Furthermore, one must proactively seek out such opportunities, rather than simply waiting for the tap on the shoulder. In the case of Tom Brady, he took a significant risk in 2020 by leaving behind a system he knew well when it became clear the Patriots were moving in a different direction. Brady joined the Tampa Bay Buccaneers and lead them to a Super Bowl championship in 2021.

The ability to recognize opportunities when they present themselves is important, but opportunities are more likely to knock on the door of those who possess the mentality to seek them out.

BEING A SLAVE TO YOUR BUSINESS PROCESSES WILL DESTROY YOU

The traditional approach to leadership development tends to focus on moving up the management ladder. High performing employees are often "rewarded" by moving them into management positions in order to move up the management hierarchy for more responsibilities. Unfortunately, the individual character traits and skill sets which propelled those individual contributors into high performers do not always align with what is needed to be an effective leader.

In most traditional organizations, important decisions on product development or investment are generally made through structured processes, such as the stage-gating process popularized by Robert Cooper over thirty years ago for product development (Cooper 1993). The stage-gating process is a project management technique in which an initiative or project is divided into distinct stages or phases, separated by decision points. Today, most research projects, product development initiatives, and capital investment decisions in large organizations are managed through some variation of the stage-gating process.

However, there is a growing recognition that the stage-gating process, while still an important foundation for the decision-making discipline, does not always adequately address today's dynamic market environment when applied blindly. In a recent webinar organized by McKinsey and the Project Production Institute, they highlighted the fundamental issues with the stage-gating process for making capital investment decisions (Arbulu, Fisher and Hartung 2021).

First of all, the pace of technology advancement and market change have increased significantly. In a fast-moving environment, speed and agility in decision-making are critical for achieving a competitive advantage. Most business decisions will need to be made without complete information. The rigor in the stage-gating process tends to lead to teams answering questions which may not always be mission critical. Instead, leaders need to take educated risks, make decisions, and learn to fail fast.

Second, the stage-gating process has the tendency of driving teams to focus on advancing to the next stage, rather than the overall business objective. For time-critical projects, focusing on the overall objective can allow for early identification of constraints and appropriate prioritization of work.

Fundamentally, the intent of the stage-gating process is to identify and manage risks by minimizing what could go wrong. The process can lead to a culture of risk aversion and tip the balance of risk-reward toward overly conservative approaches when transformational change is needed.

In the end, all processes are there to serve a business objective and not the other way around. One always needs to be cognizant of the fact that processes do not accommodate all scenarios. It is important to have the appropriate mindset to develop fit-for-purpose applications of processes. Otherwise, being a slave to the process will destroy you. In fact, the same issue is true not only for capital project decision-making but also for research projects and product development.

As an example, innovation, by its nature, is a messy process with significant uncertainty and ambiguity. A measured step-by-step process often no longer serves the business well with the increased pace of technological and business change. Instead, organizations need to focus on identification and validation of key assumptions for new ideas so they can fail fast, learn fast, and progress fast.

Anyone can identify a thousand reasons why something won't work, but it takes leadership to turn one good idea into a true innovation.

PROJECT CENTRIC LEADERSHIP

During the twentieth century, managing operations was the key to value creation through advances in efficiency and productivity. According to a recent article in Harvard Business Review (Nieto-Rodriguez 2021), there is a fundamental shift from operations to a project economy. In other words, company initiatives are increasingly driven by short-term projects through more frequent organizational changes, faster development of new products, and quicker adoption of new technologies.

During a recent interview for the book with Mr. Gary Kaplan, President of Construction at AXA XL, an American subsidiary of the global insurance company AXA, he shared with me a powerful way of thinking about the permission paradox. Other than his role at AXA XL, is also the chairman of Rapid Result Initiative (RRI), a non-profit organization which, leveraging a project approach, unleashes the power of front-line teams to create transformative impact on a variety of complex societal issues. They inspire teams to set unreasonable but believable goals and harness the intense levels of innovation, collaboration and execution required to achieve them. They pioneered the approach of one hundred-day challenges within government programs and community change efforts in more than twenty countries—including work in homelessness, healthcare, workplace safety, and criminal justice systems.

In one of the cases highlighted on its website by RRI in the Dominican Republic, RRI collaborated with the World Bank and the Instituto Técnologico de Santo Domingo (INTEC) to accelerate and deepen participative governance in the Dominican Republic (Rapid Results Institute 2022). After training sessions with INTEC and interview, two key areas of focus emerged in the justice sector—aggravated robbery and gender violence. The two teams, made up of more than fifty staff and leaders across seven institutions, set an ambitious goal for themselves—quintuple the number of aggravated robbery and gender violence cases resolved in just one hundred days. Remarkably, by day fifty of the challenge, both teams had almost achieved or exceeded their original goal. The teams responded by challenging themselves further and increasing their initial goals.

The Sustainability Review, which marked the end of the one hundred-day challenge, was attended by several dignitaries, including the Attorney General of the Dominican Republic, Dr. Jean Rodriguez, who remarked, "If we do not change, there will be no change."

The same approach is equally applicable to business initiatives. For example, a process sometimes referred to as the "sprint" is increasingly used for innovation activities in order to create clarity for specific business opportunities or technology development. In one of the sprints I personally led before my retirement, we brought eight team members from six different parts of the company with very different perspectives and different expertise for a short two-month sprint exercise. This was for a potentially important idea, but it needed a new, dedicated team because it did not fit the existing organizational structure. Prior to the sprint team forming, there had been no clear focus and no significant progress made for an extended period.

Partly due to the pandemic, the sprint team never even met in person. We had a weekly meeting led by pre-assigned sub -team leaders who shared their learnings on different aspects of the initiative such as technology, business, regulatory and opportunity assessments. We were able to quickly invalidate or confirm certain key assumptions, reconcile the different opinions by engaging both internal and external experts, and make specific recommendations for the path forward. The progress was made possible by the project-oriented team, working around the traditional organizational barriers.

There is a fundamentally different dynamic in the so-called project-centric leadership vs. organization-centric leadership.

First of all, short-duration projects generally have clearly defined and focused business objectives. It is easier to see the impact of the effort. Second, depending on the culture of organizations, one may have more flexibility and less bureaucracy to form a team. The sponsoring managers can make those decisions very quickly. In addition, the formation of a team for a short project with a defined timeline is a relatively low-risk activity for either the team leader or the business.

Typical projects consist of about 10–15 members from different organizations. Project leaders have to develop the ability to articulate a vision for the team through a sponsorship statement to define the opportunity or problem. The project leader has to advocate the proposed opportunities to stakeholders, motivate people who are not reporting to them, and influence other organizations to be on board with the mission—all necessary components for leadership development.

If you are an aspiring leader, it is important to shift your mindset from climbing the management ladder, which tends to be a very crowded and competitive space, to identifying and proactively leading team-oriented projects where you can demonstrate your leadership and quickly create business impacts with fewer bureaucratic barriers to work through.

Compared to the traditional organization-based approach, project-centric initiatives require even more focus on the ability to influence without authority, as we discussed in Chapter 4. You will most likely have more stakeholders. You will have to influence more people to buy into your ideas and visions. You will have to develop the trust and credibility of more diverse team members. It is through those efforts that you can learn leadership skills and grow into a leader.

Gary Kaplan summarized our interview by saying, "to me, that is the best development for leadership, you know, doing those projects!"

IMPLICATION

Climbing the management ladder tends to be a very crowded and competitive space. Instead, leading team-oriented projects can be a more effective route to demonstrate leadership, create business impacts, and eventually grow into a leader.

LEADERSHIP EXERCISE

Identify a specific issue either inside or outside of the workplace that you would like to pursue. Develop a one-page plan, including a clearly defined objective that is achievable in sixty days, resource the plan and explain what it would mean for the stakeholders if successful.

CHAPTER 16

THE ANSWER TO DIFFERENCE IS TO RESPECT IT

———

When people go to work, they should not have to leave their hearts at home.

—*BETTY BENDER*

"My name is Brandon Capetillo, and I am the mayor of Baytown... but I am a quality manager at Air Liquide, an industrial gas company. Mayorship is a part-time job." I can still remember the bewilderment on the face of the Chinese mayor from Huizhou when Mr. Capetillo made the introduction.

In 2018, when ExxonMobil was developing an investment project in China, I hosted the then mayor of Huizhou (a Chinese city not too far from Hong Kong). During his visit to Texas, we arranged for him to meet with the mayor of Baytown, where some of the world's largest petrochemical complexes are located.

Chinese mayors are on the front lines of the country's move toward urbanization and economic growth. The local governments are responsible for a lion's share of the country's public expenditure, including all public spending on education, health, unemployment insurance, social security, and welfare. The central government gives local governments considerable leeway in adopting policies to boost economic growth and encourages local governments to undertake approved policy experiments.

The mayor of Huizhou, a third-tier city in China but with about two and half million residents, has an extremely demanding job with many responsibilities, including personal involvement in many of the specific decisions about the investment we were negotiating. Unsurprisingly, there is a large administrative structure to support all these operations.

At the meeting, he was not only completely shocked but also puzzled by the fact the mayor of Baytown, hosting some of the world's largest petrochemical complexes, could be a part-time job. Neither side was fully digesting and appreciating the fact that the different social and cultural structures resulted in fundamentally different expectations of political leaders.

The cultural differences can create challenges in many different ways.

"Just Do It" is arguably one of the most well-known tag lines ever created. Nike has been leveraging that line, along with the famous logo, for many years. Interestingly, I have never seen that slogan in Chinese anywhere. A quick Google search did not find any official Chinese translation of that tag line.

As one of the most successful sportswear companies in the world, Nike did not simply copy and paste their successful campaign slogan in English and translate it into Chinese. The phrase is very action oriented and resonates with Americans well, and, in English, the phrase is short and punchy. However, there is simply not a good Chinese translation to capture that essence; at least I have not seen one. Instead, Nike has created several different tag lines to go with its specific marketing campaigns.

For many years, China has been one of Nike's biggest revenue drivers. As Nike CEO John Donahue noted in a 1Q2021 quarterly earnings call, "our strategy is working with business results that reflect our deep connection to consumers around the world" (Nike 2021). Nike's success in China is partly due to its localization of its business strategy. For example, leveraging China's vibrant e-commerce ecosystem, Nike achieved over 42 percent of sales through digital sales in China, vs. about 20 percent global sales (Daxueconsulting 2022).

Simply categorizing cultures as Western or Eastern is obviously a gross simplification of the complex nature of the world. However, we can still discuss the leadership implications without stereotyping.

Ever since Marco Polo visited China over a thousand years ago, there has always been a fascination with the difference between Western culture and Eastern culture. On the one hand, the Industrial Revolution propelled Europe into global leadership positions and challenged the fundamental belief of leadership-philosophy in the East, especially in China. On the other hand, the unprecedented economic development in China in the last forty years, which lifted eight hundred million people out of poverty, is creating further debate about different conceptions of leadership between the West and the East.

I will endeavor to share my perspectives on how leaders from the two different cultures think differently, which can be insightful for multinational companies operating across the globe.

LONG-TERM ORIENTATION VS. SHORT-TERM OBJECTIVES

Most Western businesses have business strategies with three-to-five-year outlooks and an annual operating plan. But companies, especially public companies, are often driven by pressure from financial institutions to perform quarterly.

From a cultural perspective, Asian cultures, in general, tend to have a longer-term orientation than what is typical of Western cultures. People are willing to delay short-term material or social success or even short-term emotional gratification in order to prepare for the future, as illustrated by the higher saving rates in China (Zhang et al. 2018). They attach great importance to the future, treat things with a dynamic perspective, and leave room for anything. They tend to value persistence, perseverance and being able to adapt.

This long-term orientation naturally leads Chinese culture to focus on long-term relationships, which is reflected in the Chinese business model, which traditionally tends to be less contractual and more based on trust and relationships. Although trust and relationships are no longer sufficient for success in the modern business environment, understanding the cultural context is still important. This long-term orientation also leads Chinese culture to value past experience more when it comes to decision-making. What happened in the past is regarded as the right judgment for the present and future. Western cultures focus much more on the present.

The combination of long-term orientation with the current blistering pace of change is creating an interesting dichotomy for many Western companies. The fast-changing nature of society in the last few decades has created a "use-it-or-lose-it" urgency for businesses to take advantage of market opportunities when they arise.

Western business leaders working in China have to figure out how to balance their long-term vision while acting with agility and a willingness to learn when it comes to specific business opportunities. It is counterintuitive, but some companies even take an approach of getting things ready while waiting for the right opportunity in order to be able to act quickly when the condition is ready. Successful leaders have to drive short-term results while at the same time rethinking strategy amid seismic shifts in the competitive environment and ways of working.

CONTEXTUAL THINKING VS. LINEAR BUSINESS PROCESS

Western analytical thinking, where one idea builds upon the other sequentially, underlies the modern scientific method and has had a significant influence on industrialization, modernization, and Western legal framework. Businesspeople are no exceptions.

One example in a business context is the stage-gating process, a project management technique in which an initiative or project is divided into distinct stages or phases, separated by decision points. It is a perfect embodiment of the linear thinking process. You often observe Western companies conduct activities in sequence while Chinese companies progress activities in parallel.

One can often note that neither side is fully aware of or appreciates the other side's style of reasoning during cross-cultural business negotiations.

Chinese culture focuses on lateral or more holistic thinking, which does not build from subject to object, but rather connects across subjects. People in more collective societies tend to be more "holistic" in the way they think about problems, focusing more on the relationships and the context of the situation at hand, while people in individualistic societies tend to focus on separate elements, and to consider situations as fixed and unchanging. Some attribute the differences to the distinction between Westerners' independent self and Easterners' interdependent self. Others attribute the difference to

Chinese philosophical tradition vs. the analytical approach from ancient Greece.

It is also interesting to note linguistic differences also mirror these cultural differences. Chinese languages are topic-prominent languages, whereas English is a subject-prominent language. According to a BBC report (Robson 2017), when asked to name the two related items in a list of words such as "train, bus, track", people in the West might pick "bus" and "train" because they are both types of vehicles. A holistic thinker, in contrast, would say "train" and "track" since they are focusing on the functional relationship.

In the West, people tend to believe in absolute truths, that ideas or actions are immutably true or false, or even good or bad. In the East, whether something is true or false, or good or bad, depends upon the context, one's point of view, and the timing. The classic yin and yang wheel, with two connected parts of a white swirl and a black swirl, signifies that everything in the universe has two opposite forces. But the whole symbol indicates the concept of interdependent and interpenetrating opposing forces to complete each other for a harmonious wholeness.

One implication in the business context is the interpretation of government policies and regulations. For Westerners, regulatory gray areas are likely to be interpreted as a reason to stop. For many Chinese companies, which grew up with nothing but gray zones, they would likely be interpreted based on the social context. Some entrepreneurs are growing fabulously wealthy by taking advantage of the gray zone before policies become mature. Some even say the lack of specificity is a feature rather than a bug to allow the necessary flexibility for the government to deal with the fact China has a wide range of development stages for different segments of the society.

How to successfully navigate the regulatory ambiguity, while avoiding the associated risks, is an important aspect of the decision-making process for Western companies. Taking a linear approach, while effective in the Western business environment, would often run into headwinds in the Asian business environment.

LEADERSHIP BEHAVIOR

In many Asian cultures, self-promotion is viewed negatively, and every culture has its own metaphor for those who are viewed as overreaching. In Japan, the nail that sticks out gets hammered down. In China, it is even worse—the bird that sticks its heads out first gets shot. For many of us who grew up in a culture which values humility and modesty, the idea of drawing attention to ourselves seems distasteful.

In American culture, it is a different story. It is branded differently, but assertive self-confidence is part of American culture, especially in the business world where everyone is conditioned to think that he or she is above average. When asked about their competence, 94 percent of American professors claimed they were better than average (Robson 2017). Even phrases such as "do not toot your own horn" are often used to humble brag, "I am not tooting my own horn but I work a lot quicker than most people."

While bragging is generally viewed as a negative quality, there is nothing wrong with giving oneself a mental pat on the back for a job well done. Recognizing your successes can help boost the feelings of self-confidence and prepare you for future successes. You don't have to always hide your light completely under a bushel.

When it comes to perceptions of leadership, humility can sometimes be perceived as a lack of leadership. I would like to share a few highlights based on a recent HBR article by Leslie John, professor at Harvard Business School. John offers excellent advice for striking a balance, embracing humility, and not being perceived as bragging (John 2021).

- *Share when asked. If someone requests information or an answer that requires you to reveal positives about yourself, you should oblige.*
- *Find a promoter. No one brings an agent to work, but you can find intermediaries, including your peers, bosses, mentors, and sponsors, who will be happy to speak on your behalf—as long as you are respectful in your solicitation.*
- *If someone unexpectedly compliments you publicly, resist the instinct to humbly downplay it; a smile or a simple thank you will suffice.*

I recently interviewed Dr. Patricia Delgado, who did her doctoral research on the influence of Hispanic culture on leadership for Hispanics in the US, especially in the context of how organizations and leaders can gain understanding and knowledge about Hispanic millennials which represent 22 percent of the millennial population and 25 percent of the Hispanic population in the United States (Delgado 2021).

"We sacrifice ourselves for the family. These millennials and Gen Zers that want to step out of the Hispanic circle, are being challenged by their own peers." Family is important in any culture, but Dr. Delgado used the example to illustrate the different implications when it comes to Hispanic millennials.

On the one hand, the culture is beautiful and does give them the beauty of family for support. On the other hand, those behaviors could be construed differently in terms of leadership and commitment to an organization. For example, if staying close to family means not being able to relocate where business needs are, it could be perceived as less committed to the organizations.

Her research was to ensure Hispanic millennials, as well as Hispanic generations after them, are not overlooked as leaders. At the same time, the purpose of the study was to increase awareness of the barriers that impede Hispanic advancement in professional and leadership positions. Obviously, she is not advocating the shedding of one's cultural background in order to succeed in business. However, understanding one's own culture and how those culturally specific values interact in the global business environment is the first step to negotiating the strengths and weaknesses of relating to others with different cultural backgrounds with regard to leadership in corporate environments.

For organizations, understanding the underlying cultural context can help uncover what effective approaches and challenges organizations and leaders will have when retaining and developing Hispanic millennials into leaders.

In summary, misconceptions and misplaced cultural assumptions continue posing challenges for organizations even as the nature of business becomes increasingly global. Geopolitical dynamics can add another layer of complexity. Yet many companies are still trying to enter, establish or expand in developing markets, hoping to get a share of the growing global middle classes, the new talent pool, and the new wave of innovations for growth.

The key to success is not to make assumptions about others' actions or motivations based on our own pre-conceived notions. Inclusive leaders must take into consideration the fundamental differences ingrained in different business cultures and develop innovative ways to make business decisions in order to have sustained success in those cultural contexts.

We must respect and account for our cultural differences. Instead of treating others how we want to be treated, we must "treat people the way *they* want to be treated," as author Simon Sinek said.

IMPLICATION

Misconceptions and misplaced cultural assumptions continue posing challenges for organizations even as the nature of business becomes increasingly global. It is not only important to understand one's own culture but also the culture of those we work with, and how those culturally specific values interact in the global business environment. We all have to take into consideration the fundamental differences ingrained in different business cultures and develop innovative ways to make business decisions in order to have sustained success in different cultural environments.

People have sometimes described culture as an iceberg, with 20 percent visible and 80 percent invisible below the water. Identify some of the cultural values or traits of your own which are invisible but can potentially affect how you lead or make decisions.

CHAPTER 17

FAILURES ARE STEPPING STONES TO SUCCESS

———

A man who has been through bitter experiences and travelled far enjoys even his sufferings after a time.

—HOMER, THE ODYSSEY

Ime Udoka, a rookie coach for the storied NBA Boston Celtics, is probably not a household name for most people, but his brilliance propelled the Boston Celtics to the 2022 NBA Finals, just short of winning a record eighteenth NBA championship. The Celtics struck gold by hiring Udoka in the offseason (Goss 2022).

A former player who had to scrape and claw for every opportunity to stay in the league, Udoka went on to be a highly regarded assistant for several years. Yet he was consistently passed over by teams with head coach vacancies.

"I can go down the list. [...] That was tough because I believe I was ready." Udoka told Yahoo Sports. Udoka was an assistant coach with three different organizations before the Celtics entrusted him the role at the age of forty-three. The path to success for Udoka was a challenging one and each rejection was a disappointment, but he took the process in stride and looked inward.

"You try to improve and you get feedback from the interviews and what your weaknesses are perceived as," he reflected to Yahoo Sports. "I think for me, it's easy. My career as a player, a journeyman, a role player that only had two guaranteed contracts out of my whole NBA career, it prepped me for that. It's always been about putting your head down and grinding it out and figuring out a way to get it done. You don't place the blame on anybody or any situation. You figure out how to get it done. That's what I try to really impart on the team, but for me it's, shake it off and keep it moving."

Just as I was finishing up the book, there was an unexpected turn of events for both Udoka and the Celtics. He was suspended by the Celtics for the whole 2022 season due to an undisclosed inappropriate workplace relationship. The story just further illustrates the responsibility and obligation leaders have to act ethically toward others as well as the organization, as we discussed in Chapter 2.

As a leader, Udoka was not only responsible for himself, his family, but he had an awesome responsibility for the young Celtics team, which was on the verge of achieving greatness. Instead, his personal indiscretion not only damaged his relationship with his family, setback or even derailed his career, but also created significant challenges for the Celtics organization when leadership was needed the most. It is unclear if he will ever have a chance to lead the Celtics team again, but I hope he will learn from his mistake and recover as a leader. As it is popularly said, it is not how you fall but how you recover that matters.

Successes are cause for celebration, but failures are rarely shared or talked about. The road to success is littered with failures, and aspiring leaders have to be able to face rejection with a positive mentality. In fact, Former British Prime Minister Tony Blair once said, "The art of leadership is saying no, not saying yes. It is very easy to say yes."

Venture capitalists turn down over 95 percent of applicants before they choose to invest. Ivy League schools reject over 90 percent of their applicants each year. Chances are, if you had not pursued the career, contest, or relationship, you wouldn't have experienced rejection. But you wouldn't have completely experienced life either. Learn to see rejection as proof that you're brave enough to take on risks and to participate in the wide realm of experiences available on this planet. Feel empowered by what you have accomplished.

Here is a quote attributed to author Steve Maraboli. "As I look back to my life, I realize that every time I thought I was rejected by something good, I was actually re-directed to something better." What a positive way to look at life! It is a perfect articulation of how life is less about what happens to you, but more about how you react to it. I am sure all of us have had disappointments from being rejected in our lives or careers and often thought about the could-have and would-have, but the way Maraboli describes rejection allows us to have a whole new perspective. More importantly, failure is the fastest way to learn.

I have relocated many times since I came to the US over thirty years ago. With each move, we donated, recycled, or threw away many of the things we accumulated. For no particular reason, I have always kept a stack of over one hundred rejection letters when I first started looking for employment in the US after I completed my doctorate degree at MIT, including rejection letters from both Exxon and Mobil, the predecessors of ExxonMobil where I worked for the past sixteen years.

Long before those rejection letters, I experienced many setbacks, each of which could have been a life-changing event. I did not get into college on my first try in 1977 after high school and had to work on a farm for another year before I was accepted to college the following year. I did not pass my graduate school exam after college and worked in a local government office for a year before I went to graduate school the following year. I was getting ready for a PhD program in Japan, but my application was rejected at the last minute before MIT accepted me the subsequent year.

Such is my journey, but I suppose many of you have had similar experiences in life. It is the tortuous path of life that makes life interesting, meaningful, and rewarding. I do not necessarily consider my life unique or different, but it has been very rewarding. Fighting through adversity and battles just puts pages in the book of our life journeys. Embracing the risk of rejection allows for greater foresight and forethought as we look ahead and brace ourselves for encounters with any hurdles that lie before us. Rejection doesn't necessarily mean you are not good enough. It could just mean the other person failed to realize what you have to offer.

In expanding Wayne Gretzky's quote, "you miss 100 percent of the shots you never take," Jared Diamond made the following analogy about risk taking in his book, *The World Until Yesterday, What Can We Learn from Traditional Societies?* (Diamond 2012).

"My New Guinea friends would understand Gretzky's quip, and would add two footnotes to it. First, a closer analogy with traditional life would be if you were actually penalized for missing a shot—but you would still take shots, albeit more cautiously. Second, a hockey player can't wait forever for the perfect opportunity to take a shot, because a hockey game has a time limit for one hour. Similarly, traditional lives include time limits; you will die of thirst within a few days if you don't take risks in finding water, you will starve within a few weeks if you don't take risks in obtaining food, and you will die within less than a century no matter what you do."

Every single one of us has had to fight battles to get from where we were to where we are. Life is not a matter of holding good cards, but of playing a poor hand well. The key is to have clarity on the alignment of your pursuit with your fundamental values and purposes. Never give up as long as the pursuits are motivated by the right reasons—positive motivations like your dreams; your passions; the want to help people, your country, or provide a secure future for your family. When you are motivated by the right reasons, the temptation to quit will quickly subside.

There is no such thing as a failure. There is either success or lessons learned. I am very thankful of the way my parents raised me to appreciate working hard and being positive. Always be willing to learn. Be inspired and fueled by others' success, but do not allow yourself to get derailed or thrown off the path by bumps on the journey. Stay positive and stay focused. The best route to fulfillment in life is often the path of more resistance.

When Professor Amy Edmondson was describing failures in businesses at a forum organized by *FAIL! Inspiring Resilience*, she described the concept of preventable failures vs intelligent failures (FAIL! Inspiring Resilience 2019). While preventable failures obviously should be minimized, intelligent failures should be an expected result of the normal framework of business decisions as long as the failures are associated smart hypotheses. The key is to have a clear sight of the reason you are taking the risk. In fact, business innovation inherently needs more intelligent failures. That means it is important to have smart hypotheses and test them. That is how organizations fail fast, learn fast, make decisions fast, and eventually succeed.

Leadership development should follow a similar mindset. Taking calculated risks is a part of life and a part of growth. A study done at the Society of Asian Scientists and Engineers concluded that aversion to risk-taking in business and careers is one of the common factors which constrains the leadership potential for many Asian professionals (Hirotsu 2021). My personal experience also suggests that willingness to take up unconventional assignments, while risky, often creates career or leadership opportunities along the way.

Achieving personal success is one thing, but sustaining that success can also be difficult. We need to continue to feed our aspiration and reignite our desire but more importantly, we must continuously reconnect with our leadership values and purpose.

As a long-time runner who has been running a marathon every year since 2009, I will explain this sentiment from a runner's perspective.

"The journey is the reward" read a sign I saw in The Woodlands Waterway in 2017 near The Woodlands Mall in Houston, Texas.

That simple phrase really epitomizes everything about my marathon training.

To run a marathon, you do not need to be an exceptional athlete, you just need to have dedication. You are running against yourself, not somebody else. You always focus on improving against yourself, not to break any records. The best thing about running is that you can never be too old to be a runner. Ms. Harriette Thompson of San Diego became the oldest woman to complete a marathon a few years ago when she finished the San Diego Marathon at the age of ninety-two (McLaughlin 2015). She recently became the oldest person to ever finish a half marathon in three hours, forty-two minutes, fifty-six seconds. I plan to run as long as I can.

It turns out that our careers, including leadership development, are just like running. Focusing on specific goals can be tiresome and striving for the sense of accomplishment can be very short lived and fleeting. The journey itself is the reward.

I will end with a popular song by Andy Love: "It's not until you fall that you fly. When your dreams come alive, you're unstoppable. Take a shot, chase the sun, find the beautiful. We will glow in the dark turning dust to gold. And we'll dream it possible."

IMPLICATION

Successes are cause for celebration, but rejections are rarely shared or talked about. While preventable failures should be minimized, intelligent failures should be part of the normal framework for business decisions as long as the failures are associated smart hypotheses.

LEADERSHIP EXERCISE

Play out slowly the events from a recent "failure" you encountered, preferably something from your workplace. Process what went wrong and write out the three things you learned from that experience.

PART VI

CONCLUSION

CHAPTER 18

LEADERSHIP SURVEY ANALYSES

The world cannot be understood without numbers. But the world cannot be understood with numbers alone.

—HANS ROSLING

This book drew heavily from my own personal experiences of triumph and struggle as a global business executive. Many of the stories include firsthand experiences or personal observations of how other leaders make decisions and lead teams or organizations. However, I did not want the book to be constrained or potentially biased by my own personal experience.

In addition to the insights drawn from personal interviews and from the two hundred seventy thousand followers of my LinkedIn leadership blogs who have provided constant inspiration for the book, I also developed a leadership survey (https://www.onbecomingaleader.net/survey) to reach an even broader community to solicit their input.

The purpose of the survey was to better understand the challenges facing aspiring leaders and their perspectives about leadership so the book can be more relevant to their needs. More specifically, the survey provides a foundation to semi-quantitatively validate some of my hypotheses and assumptions about leadership development.

At the same time, the insights and feedback from the survey can provoke discussions and provide unbiased data to guide both individuals and organizations to make decisions. The survey will not end with the book. Instead, I am hoping more people will continue participating in the survey as a result of the book so the learning process can continue.

The survey focuses on the following aspects of leadership:
- Why do you want to be a leader?
- What defines leadership?
- What are the key roles for leaders?
- What makes great leaders?
- What are the biggest organizational barriers for aspiring leaders?
- What are the key success factors for aspiring leaders?
- What are the deadly sins for aspiring leaders?
- What are the most effective options for the development of aspiring leaders?

At the time the chapter is being written, I received about five hundred sixty responses from around the world. The sample size is still relatively small to draw firm conclusions. In addition, the survey did not necessarily have the scientific rigor for representation. However, the emerging patterns still provide valuable insights for us to learn.

Before I dive into the details of the survey results, I would like to share my summary of the key learnings and insights:

- Consistent with the hypothesis that organizations do not spend enough time and effort in understanding what motivates their aspiring leaders, less than 40 percent of people were asked by their respective organizations why they want to be leaders. As a result, leadership programs are often driven by organizational objectives, which may or may not always connect or resonate with individual leaders.

- All successful organizations have to deliver on organizational objectives. However, the responses overwhelmingly list "inspire and develop people" as the top priority for leaders. These are not necessarily contradictory. Sustainable results will always need to have motivated people.

- The survey suggests that most people consider the key success factors for aspiring leaders are their ability to authentically establish trust and connect with people, through empathy, effective communication, and self-awareness. Trust, a seemingly abstract concept, is critical for leaders to forge genuine bonds. High-trust environments allow people to be their true selves. When people can bring their whole selves to work, they are not only more creative, but more productive as well. This is especially true during times of crisis, as we are currently going through with the pandemic.

- Similarly, as a leader, putting one's personal interests ahead of those of the team is the fastest way to lose trust. Putting self-interest ahead of the team came out clearly as the top deadly sin for aspiring leaders. Micromanagement and indecision follow as the next two on the list.

- Finally, consistent with the hypotheses that leadership starts with self-awareness, the survey response ranked self-reflection as the most effective option for the development of aspiring leaders, followed by mentoring and coaching. The survey results validated my intuition when I started the book and helped me clarify and crystallize the focus of the book should be on self-discovery and self-awareness. With the right approach, self-reflection and mentoring programs can be effective and offer better return on investment than many formal corporate leadership programs.

Here is a more detailed breakdown of the results:

DEMOGRAPHICS

REGION
Most of the responses were from North America. However, I am very encouraged by the participation from all around the world. The survey includes responses from all regions in the world with North America at about 49 percent, EU and Asia/Pacific each about 13 percent, 6 percent from Africa, and the rest from the Middle East and South America. While different cultures might have different perspectives on what leadership means, there is a universal hunger for authentic leadership learnings and insights.

ROLE OF RESPONDENTS
Survey respondents include about 9 percent from the C-suite level, 28 percent from senior level management classified as VP/Director, 44 percent from junior level management

including manager, supervisor, team leader. The remaining 19 percent described themselves as individual contributors. It is interesting to note the majority of the participants are already in various of leadership positions in their organizations, rather than people who are just aspiring to be leaders.

YEARS OF LEADERSHIP EXPERIENCE

In terms of leadership experience, the distribution was relatively even among early career, mid-career, and late-career with 27 percent with 0–5 years of leadership experience, 21 percent with 5–10 years, 27 percent with 10–20 years and 25 percent with over 20 years of leadership experience. I believe the distribution is a reflection of the fact that leadership development never stops and is indeed a journey throughout one's career.

WHY DO YOU WANT TO BE A LEADER?

While 82 percent of respondents stated they had asked themselves the question about why they wanted to be leaders, only 39 percent of the responses stated their organizations ever asked the same question! It is consistent with the hypothesis that organizations do not spend enough time and effort in understanding what motivates their aspiring leaders. As a result, leadership programs are often driven by organizational objectives, which may or may not always resonate with personal leadership values. Unless organizations better understand what really motivates people to be leaders, they will continue having challenges energizing organizations and developing the next generation of leaders.

WHAT DEFINES LEADERSHIP?

On the question of what defines leadership, the survey was open-ended and asked people to provide three words which they thought best define leadership. The responses highlighted the foundation of leadership is one's character, including integrity, honesty, perseverance, and authenticity. However, leadership is also a combination of one's character, competence, and leadership behavior. As expected, the results are wide ranging, but some interesting patterns emerge.

Here are the top fifteen words they shared in order or frequency of appearance:

Vision, inspire, servant leadership, empathy, support, role model, integrity, mentor, direction, listener, motivator, lead, influence, communicator, empower.

The overwhelming response implies that people are looking for inspiration and vision from leaders. They are expecting leaders to inspire, support, and provide development opportunities for the growth of the next generation of leaders. It does not mean people do not care about business results or organizational objectives. However, it does demand leaders to balance delivering business results and developing people.

WHAT ARE THE KEY ROLES FOR LEADERS?

Please state whether readers agree or disagree with the following statements.

Strongly agree: 2; Agree: 1; Neutral: 0; Disagree: -1; Strongly Disagree: -2

Here is the average response:

The most important function for a leader is to inspire and develop people	1.73
The most important function for a leader is to develop organization culture	1.32
The most important function for a leader is to create vision for an organization	1.18
The most important function for a leader is to deliver on organizations objectives	0.91

All of the four prescribed roles are obviously important for any leader. You cannot have a successful organization without having leaders who can create vision, deliver on organizational objectives, develop culture, and inspire/develop people. It is worth noting "inspiration and people development" came out as the most important key role according to the survey results.

WHAT MAKES GREAT LEADERS?
Similar to the above questions, I asked readers to state whether they agree or disagree with statements about what makes great leaders.

Strongly agree: 2; Agree: 1; Neutral: 0; Disagree: -1; Strongly Disagree: -2

Values (e.g., Integrity, Honesty, Trust)	1.75
Character (e.g., Passion, Courage, Beliefs, Decisiveness)	1.6
Skills (e.g., Empathy, Communication, Technical Expertise, Negotiation Skill)	1.45

Skills are important, but leadership values and character are rated higher. Many corporate leadership programs focus on leadership skills, rather than devoting the effort to understand how to align values. The question for organizations is how do you focus on values and character development for aspiring leaders?

WHAT ARE THE BIGGEST ORGANIZATIONAL BARRIERS FOR ASPIRING LEADERS?

Lack of mentor/coach	18.9%
Lack of inclusive culture	15.4%
Lack of honest feedbacks	14.6%
Lack of trust	13.3%
Lack of leadership opportunities	12.7%
Lack of leadership training	11.8%
Lack of role model	9.8%
Lack of network	4.2%

Based on the response, lack of mentor/sponsor/coach and lack of inclusive culture were perceived to be two of the largest organizational barriers for leadership development. The two are somewhat related. On the one hand, the response suggests cookie-cutter leadership programs do not effectively address the individual needs of every aspiring leader and do not always connect individual leadership values with organizational objectives. At the same time, the standard leadership development process can reinforce unconscious biases, rather than create a more inclusive work culture, as we discussed in Chapter 10.

WHAT ARE THE KEY SUCCESS FACTORS FOR ASPIRING LEADERS?

Communication skills	18.2%
Interpersonal skills and empathy	17.7%
Adapting to change	15.8%
Self-awareness	9.2%
Trustworthiness	8.2%
People management experience	7.0%
Energy and enthusiasm	6.4%

The survey suggests the key success factors for aspiring leaders are their ability to authentically connect with people through showing empathy, good communication skills, and good self-awareness. They are also those who can adapt to change.

WHAT ARE THE DEADLY SINS FOR ASPIRING LEADERS?

Put self-interest ahead of the team	18.4%
Micromanage rather than empowering teams	13.5%
Afraid of making decisions to avoid failures	12.1%
Failure to take responsibilities when things go wrong	7.8%
Failure to hold people accountable	7.8%
Focusing on being right rather than influencing decisions for outcome	7.3%
Waiting to be empowered rather than taking ownership	7.2%

Put self-interest ahead of the team. The fastest way to lose credibility is to not walk the walk.

Micromanage rather than empowering teams. Employees who feel their voice is heard at work are 4.6 times more likely to feel empowered to perform their best work (Beheshti 2019).

Afraid of making decisions to avoid failures. Not taking risks is the riskiest career move of all. As discussed in Chapter 9, how often in our lives have we been hampered by imaginary constraints and fears?

Failure to take responsibilities when things go wrong. If you don't take responsibility, trust with your team will suffer very quickly. Your integrity and credibility are your most important assets. They are powerful when developed, but devastating once you lose them.

Failure to hold people accountable. Accountability is not simply admitting wrong and taking the blame. It is about delivering on a commitment. Fostering accountability requires clarity of expectations, capability, measurement, with clear consequences. If you do not know where you are going, you will end up somewhere else. That is true for individuals as well as organizations.

Focusing on being right rather than influencing decisions for outcome. You gain nothing by saying "I told you so." Think about Aristotle's framework for persuasion and how to establish credibility.

Waiting to be empowered rather than taking ownership. Think about the two-circle theory of leadership and the elephant story. Don't let the tiny rope on the elephant become a constraint in what you should pursue and what you could achieve.

WHAT ARE THE MOST EFFECTIVE OPTIONS FOR THE DEVELOPMENT OF ASPIRING LEADERS?

Self-reflection	20.3%
Coaching/Mentoring	19.0%
Performance feedback	15.1%
On-the-job training	13.1%
Formal leadership training program	12.6%
Assignment on challenging project	11.4%
Reading	5.7%

Consistent with the hypotheses that leadership starts with self-awareness, the survey responses listed self-reflection as the most effective option for the development of aspiring leaders, followed by mentoring and coaching.

There are different methods for self-reflection, but the key is to develop a habit so that it becomes part of the routine for replaying events in our brain. For example, I tend to block a fixed time on my calendar every Friday for structured reflection without being interrupted by meetings and emails. What were the key events of the week? What went well and what did not? What were the key learnings and what I could have done differently? I also write down the key learnings so I can refer back later.

At a team level, I always remember an experience I had thirty years ago when working on a project for a Japanese company near Tokyo. During my two weeks stay there, the team always spent about fifteen minutes every morning to go through what the key activities for the day were. Before the end of the day, the team again spent about thirty minutes to go through what happened in that day and share any key learnings. Although it was more for planning and operational purposes, the exercises forced everyone to reflect on the key events and learnings of the day at a team level.

With the right approach, mentoring programs can be both effective and have better results than many formal corporate leadership programs. A recent Harvard Business Review article (Sandvik 2022) on mentoring included an example of mentoring at a US call center, which generated an estimated 870 percent return on investment. However, mentoring programs in most companies are still ad hoc and improvised.

Aspiring leaders have to be proactive in seeking out mentors and coaches, rather than hoping corporate leadership programs will magically make you a leader. The same HBR article shared two interesting observations: the mentoring program in the study needed to be mandatory to be effective. Since it is often not practical to offer mentoring to everyone, the challenge for organizations is to figure out who needs mentoring. Another observation from the same study suggests "the people least in need of mentoring are the ones who seek it," says Christopher Stanton, one of the study authors. In the end, the success of mentoring programs often depends on the preparedness of the mentees.

From an organizational perspective, significant shifts must be made to design leadership development programs in a way that truly connect organizational objectives with individual leadership values. Such solutions would require organizations to place a greater emphasis on inclusive leadership through role-specific resources and information.

Organizations have to be thoughtful in structuring mentoring programs and be cognizant of unconscious bias in soliciting or providing mentoring support. In addition, structured training for mentees to better take advantage of any mentoring relationship could be an effective way to strengthen the effectiveness of mentoring programs.

This survey was not intended to come up a magic solution for organizations. However, the results do suggest there are opportunities for organizations to strengthen mentoring programs in a more organized and structured way. A strong mentoring program is more likely to provide insights on how to align organizational objectives with personal leadership values and purpose, resulting in more inspired and motivated leaders.

I will end with some corporate mission statements which seem to reflect the criticality of people in order for the organization to succeed. How well can business translate those mission statements into practice is the challenging part.

Microsoft's mission statement is "**to empower every person and every organization on the planet to achieve more.**"

At Marriott, "**If you take care of your associates, they will take care of the customers and the customers will come back.**"

The mission statement of Johnson & Johnson is "**to stimulate everyone and incorporate the efforts of all like-minded** individuals across the globe to join the Johnson & Johnson course of impacting the world through developmental deeds."

Goldman Sachs Businesses Principle: "**We have yet to find the limits to the responsibility our best people are able to assume.**"

IMPLICATION

Aspiring leaders should not solely rely on their organizations for their own leadership development. It is their own journey, and they have to take ownership. At the same time, the survey results suggest companies need to do a better job in connecting organizational objectives with what truly motivates people.

LEADERSHIP EXERCISE

Identify the biggest barriers to your leadership development in your organization. Develop a six-month action plan based on your assessment of the most effective option to enhance your leadership.

If you have not done so, please take five minutes to fill out the leadership survey by visiting:
https://www.onbecomingaleader.net/survey.

CHAPTER 19

PERSONAL LEADERSHIP IMPLICATIONS

If your actions inspire others to dream more, learn more, do more and become more, you are a leader.

—JOHN QUINCY ADAMS

If you visit Joshua Tree National Park in Southern California, you would likely be amazed by the unusual, mysterious, other-worldly looking Joshua trees. Joshua trees grow as a vertical stem with no branches for the first few decades of their life until the first blossoms appear. After the blossoms drop off, new leaves grow beneath this dead portion and a new branch begins its growth, expanding rigidly in a totally different direction. Each branching stem also abruptly ends its growth after blossoming, and further branches veer off in new directions. After many years, Joshua trees develop a complex system of twisted branches growing in many directions. Adding to the intricacy, Joshua trees are top-heavy, and they are often wind-blown and tilted over due to the high winds in the barren environments they live in.

The balance between this unique growth pattern and the struggle against gravity and wind is the secret to the individuality of each Joshua tree's grotesque yet beautiful appearance. Our personal leadership journey follows a very similar pattern, mysterious, sometimes unpredictable, and a product of our resilience. It is the individual struggle which makes everyone unique and life beautiful.

I am hoping that reading my book, along with the insights you gained through the leadership exercises in each chapter, will help you find your own unique growth pattern and endure your own leadership struggles. Each individual will probably internalize the concepts differently depending on their own circumstance or individual needs. Upon reading the frameworks in this book, you can and will reach the appropriate leadership decisions on your own. You can answer your own leadership questions more insightfully than I ever could. You have to find clarity about your own leadership values from the complexity of the practical world.

Through that process, you find ways to ignite your inner spark and generate your own sources of fortitude and purpose. For example, if you feel you need to have more focus on understanding others rather than focusing your own view, you can decide before any engagement what percentage of time you want to be talking vs. asking questions and listening. If you feel you're often afraid of making tough decisions, try to think about the cost of indecision. Having a plan B is fine, but be willing to make decisions and commit. Arnold Schwarzenegger once said, "every thought you put into Plan B is energy you are taking away from Plan A."

Studying what great leaders do can offer us a window onto the wider world, broaden our perspective and open our eyes to new wonders. However, one cannot expect to have great results simply by imitating what other leaders do. We do not want to be constricted by preset ideas, thereby forestalling the possibility of new discoveries and missing the possibility of seeing the unexpected.

Likewise, you should not solely rely on your organization for your own leadership development. It is your journey, and you have to take ownership of your leadership development. Many companies embrace in their mission and vision statements that their people come first. However, regardless of what organizations say, it does not always play out as intended when those statements are put to test in actual practices. When it comes to individual leadership development, you have to personalize how to adapt your own individual leadership values to align with the organization's purpose and objective.

As you grow as a leader, you will develop more conviction and resilience. The alignment of your personal values and your organization's values can help drive your passion, courage, resilience, and conviction. It is when people say, "when you love your job you never work a day in your life."

Finally, a leader needs to have the proper skills to succeed. With the dynamic and fast-changing business environment we are in today and the expectation today that everyone being a leader, the key is not to expect leaders to already have all the necessary arrows in their quivers in terms of skill sets but rather to have an open mind and be willing to learn.

Regardless of where you are in the world, there is a risk in being ignorant, but there is no risk in being humble. People with an open mind are likely to have a better chance to formally or informally access and synthesize new information, connecting with something they had experience with, to develop a new mental framework for making the right decisions. Clarity on leadership insights often comes at some moments in which the perfect set of circumstances trigger an epiphany that alters the way you think. Once you develop the mental clarity on the opportunities for your leadership development, it is simply a matter of making it a habit by being more intentional.

Whenever you get an insight so powerful it becomes a defining principle, it will give you a new perspective for guiding future decisions. The new, uncertain world of today requires leaders to recognize their old mental models may no longer be relevant or effective, and they need to continue learning and unlearning in order to be effective.

Find your own unique path. Control your own destiny. Set ambitious goals but enjoy the journey. Listen to many, but decide on your own. No one knows what's best for you than you. No one else can understand your internal motivations for why you do what you do.

On this journey of leadership growth, we learn many lessons: how to know ourselves better, how to lead effectively, and how to make decisions based on a vision for the future. Everyone's learning path will be different. I fundamentally believe everyone has the potential to lead, but the true challenge is for organizations to provide the opportunity and environment for everybody to develop their own personalized leadership style, and for individuals to put in the hard work.

After all, Vince Lombardi already told us a long time ago, "leaders aren't born, they are made. And they are made just like anything else, through hard work."

APPENDIX A
REFERENCES

———

INTRODUCTION

Andrews, Margaret. 2016. "Teaching Leadership for Change in Business School." *University Worlds News.* May 27. *https://www.universityworldnews.com/post. php?story=20160524205146492.*

Gurdjian, Pierre, Thomas Halbeisen, and Kevin Lane. 2014. "Why Leadership-Development Programs Fail." *McKinsey Quarterly.* *https://www.mckinsey.com/featured-insights/leadership/why-leadership-development-programs-fail.*

Kamkwamba, William and Bryan Mealer. 2010. *The Boy Who Harnessed the Wind: Creating Currents of Electricity and Hope (illustrated edition).* New York: HarperCollins Publishers.

Moving Windmills Project. 2022. "Moving Windmills Project, Inspiring African Innovation." *Moving Windmills.* *https://movingwindmills.org*

Sinek, Simon. 2011. *Start with Why: How Great Leaders Inspire Everyone to Take Action.* New York, NY: Portfolio/Penguin.

Training Industry. 2022. "The Leadership Training Market," *https://trainingindustry.com/wiki/leadership/the-leadership-training-market.*

CHAPTER 1

Bogage, Jacob and Christian Davenport. 2022. "SpaceX Fires Workers Who Criticized Elon Musk in Open Letter." *Washington Post.* June 7. *https://www.washingtonpost.com/business/2022/06/17/spacex-workers-fired-elon-musk.*

Christensen, Clayton, James Allworth, and Karen Dillon. 2012. *How Will You Measure Your Life?* New York, NY: Harper Business.

Cook, Tim. 2017. "MIT Grads: How Will You Serve Humanity?"*MIT News On Campus and Around The World.* June 9. *https://news.mit.edu/2017/commencement-day-0609.*

Cook, Tim. 2019. "Commencement Address by Apple CEO Tim Cook ." *Stanford News, June 16. https://news.stanford.edu/2019/06/16/remarks-tim-cook-2019-stanford-commencement.*

Hagerty, James. 2020. "Harvard Professor Clayton M. Christensen Turned His Life Into a Case Study." *Wall Street Journal, January 24. https://www.wsj.com/articles/harvard-professor-clayton-m-christensen-turned-his-life-into-a-case-study-11579909615.*

CHAPTER 2

Wu, Yuwen. 2017. "China's Class of 1977: I Took an Exam That Changed China."BBC News, December 14. https://www.bbc.com/news/world-asia-china-42135342.

Li, Peng. 2022. 1977年邓小平决策恢复高考始末. *Sina News.* May 24.

http://news.sina.com.cn/c/nd/2017-05-24/doc-ifyfqqyh8183000.shtml

Thompson, Marcus. 2022. "Steph Curry's Leadership Put to the Ultimate Test After Draymond Green Incident: Thompson." The Athletic, October 7, 2022. https://theathletic.com/3666894/2022/10/07/stephen-curry-draymond-green-leadership.

CHAPTER 3

UF Herbert Wertheim College of Engineering, 2012. "Leadership Interview - William Cirioli - B.S. CHE '80." Apr 13, 2012. https://www.youtube.com/watch?v=bfbHIC-EI2w.

CHAPTER 4

Eurich, Tasha. 2018. "What Self-Awareness Really Is (and How to Cultivate It)." Harvard Business Review, January 4. https://hbr.org/2018/01/what-self-awareness-really-is-and-how-to-cultivate-it.

Hurley, Michael. 2020. "Rob Manfred's Ruling on Astros' Cheating Scheme Had One Insane Conclusion." CBS News, January 14. https://www.cbsnews.com/boston/news/rob-manfred-ruling-astros-cheating-scheme-one-insane-conclusion.

Kobe Tong, Kobe. 2022. "Best Football Fair Play? Denmark Player Deliberately Missed a Penalty in 2003." GiveMeSport, September 28. https://www.givemesport.com/88065220-best-football-fair-play-denmark-player-deliberately-missed-a-penalty-in-2003.

Trompenaars, Fons. 1998. Riding the Waves of Culture: Understanding Cultural Diversity in Business. New York, NY: McGraw-Hill.

CHAPTER 5

Garvey, Marianne. 2022. "'Wonder Years' Star Danica McKellar Explains Why She Became a Mathematician and Stopped Acting." CNN Entertainment, August 18, 2022. https://www.cnn.com/2022/08/18/entertainment/danica-mckellar-mathematician/index.htm.

NBC Sports. 2019. "Matthew Emmons, Olympic Champion Shooter, Retires With Three Medals." NBC Sports, September 11. https://olympics.nbcsports.com/2019/09/11/matt-emmons-retires-shooting.

Sheffield, Rob. 2016. "100 Greatest TV Shows of All Time." Rolling Stone, September 21. https://www.rollingstone.com/tv-movies/tv-movie-lists/100-greatest-tv-shows-of-all-time-105998.

CHAPTER 6

Dow, Jameon. 2021. "VW CEO Herbert Diess Invites Elon Musk to Talk on How Tesla Innovates Quickly." Electrek, October 16. https://electrek.co/2021/10/16/vw-ceo-herbert-diess-invites-elon-musk-to-talk-on-how-tesla-innovates-quickly.

Jordan, John. 2003. "Kennedy's Romantic Moon and Its Rhetorical Legacy for Space Exploration." *Rhetoric & Public Affairs* 6, no. 2: 209–231.

Than, Griesham. 2021. "An Ingenious Way to Run Faster." *BBC News REEL*, August 4. https://www.bbc.com/reel/playlist/the-science-of-fitness?vpid=po9r61yn.

World Economic Forum. 2020. "The Global Risks Report 2020." 15th Edition. https://www3.weforum.org/docs/WEF_Global_Risk_Report_2020.pdf.

Zetlin, Minda. 2022. "In Just 3 Words, Google CEO Sundar Pichai Taught a Leadership Lesson to Every CEO." *Inc.*, July 15. https://www.inc.com/minda-zetlin/google-ceo-sundar-pichai-memo-hiring-slowdown-inspiration.html.

CHAPTER 7

De Geus, Arie. 2002. *The Living Company: Habits for Survival in a Turbulent Business Environment*. Boston, MA: Harvard Business School Press.

Edwards, Chris. 2022. "Kongo Gumi, Established in 578AD, Is the Oldest, Continually Operating Company in the World." https://authorchrisedwards.com/2020/02/27/oldest-companies.

Grove, Andrew. 1999. *Only the Paranoid Survive: How to Exploit the Crisis Points That Challenge Every Company*. New York, NY: Currency.

Handscomb, Christopher and Shail Thaker, 2018, "Activate Agility: The
    Five Avenues to Success." McKinsey Report, February 1.
    https://www.mckinsey.com/capabilities/people-and-organization-
    al-performance/our-insights/the-organization-blog/activate-agility-
    get-these-five-things-right.

Hillenbrand, Philipp, Dieter Kiewell, Rory Miller-Cheevers, Ivan Ostojic,
    and Gisa Springer. 2019. "Traditional Company, New Business:
    The Paring That Can Ensure an Incumbent's Survival." McKinsey
    Report.
    https://www.mckinsey.com/industries/oil-and-gas/our-insights/
    traditional-company-new-businesses-the-pairing-that-can-en-
    sure-an-incumbents-survival.

Hutchinson, Martin. 2020. "How Jack Welch Destroyed Sloan's Century."
    Global Policy Institute, March 12.
    https://globalpi.org/research/how-jack-welch-destroyed-sloans-century.

Johns Hopkins Applied Physics Laboratory. 2022. "Critical Contributions
    to Critical Challenges." Accessed on September 22, 2022.
    https://www.jhuapl.edu.

Leger, Justin. 2022. "KG's influence remains strong in Celtics locker
    room." NBC Sports, April 13.
    https://www.nbcsports.com/boston/celtics/kevin-garnetts-influence-
    remains-strong-celtics-locker-room.

Stewart, Jim. 2017. "Did the Jack Welch Model Sow Seeds of G.E.'s
    Decline?" New York Times, June 15.
    https://www.nytimes.com/2017/06/15/business/ge-jack-welch-immelt.html.

Sydell, Laura. 2012. "Intel Legends Moore and Grove: Making It Last."
   NPR Morning Edition, April 6.
   https://www.npr.org/2012/04/06/150057676/intel-legends-moore-and-
   grove-making-it-last.

Takubo, Yoshihiko. 2022. "Japanese Values & Longevity: The Oldest
   Companies in the World." GLOBIS Insights, August 16.
   https://globisinsights.com/purpose/values/japanese-values-
   drive-oldest-companies-in-the-world.

CHAPTER 8

Bryar, Colin and Bill Carr. 2021. *Working Backwards: Insights, Stories,*
   and Secrets from Inside Amazon. New York, NY: St. Martin's Press.

Dean, Sam. 2021. "The Real Story Behind a Tech Founder's 'Tweetstorm
   That Saves Christmas." Los Angeles Times, October 28.
   https://www.latimes.com/business/technology/story/2021-10-28/the-
   real-story-behind-a-tech-founders-tweetstorm-that-saved-christmas.

Kimmelman, Michael. 2022. "How Houston Is Fixing Homelessness."
   New York Times. June 14.
   https://www.nytimes.com/interactive/2022/06/16/headway/hous-
   ton-homeless.html.

McChrystal, Stanley, Tantum Collins, David Silverman, and Chris Fus-
   sell. 2015. Team of Teams: New Rules of Engagement for a Complex
   World. New York, NY: Portfolio/Penguin.

Nason, Rick. 2017. *It's Not Complicated: The Art and Science of Com-*
   plexity in Business. Toronto, Canada: University of Toronto Press.

Rosling, Hans, Anna Rosling Rönnlund, and Ola Rosling. 2020. *Factfulness: Ten Reasons We're Wrong About the World—and Why Things
Are Better Than You Think.* New York, NY: Flatiron Books.

Tedlow, Richard. 2006. *Andy Grove: The Life and Times of An American.*
New York, NY: Portfolio/Penguin.

CHAPTER 9

McCracken, Harry. 2017. "How the Dumpling Democratized Emoji." *Fast
Company.* August 10.
https://www.fastcompany.com/90136118/how-the-dumpling-democ-
ratized-emoji.

CHAPTER 10

Belluck, Pam. 2015. "Chilly at Work? Office Formula Was Design for
Men." *New York Times.* August 3.
https://www.nytimes.com/2015/08/04/science/chilly-at-work-a-
decades-old-formula-may-be-to-blame.html.

Cha, Ariana Eunjung. 2015. "Your Office Thermostat Is Set for Men's
Comfort. Here Is the Scientific Proof." *Washington Post.* August 3.
https://www.washingtonpost.com/news/to-your-health/
wp/2015/08/03/your-office-thermostat-is-set-for-mens-comfort-heres-
the-scientific-proof.

Davis, Leslie and Richard Fry, 2019. "College Faculty Have Become
More Racially and Ethnically Diverse, but Remain Far Less So Than
Students." *Pew Research Center.* July 31.
https://www.pewresearch.org/fact-tank/2019/07/31/us-college-fac-
ulty-student-diversity.

Hunt, Dame Vivial, Dennis Layton, and Sra Prince, 2015. "Why Diversity Matters." *McKinsey Report*, January 1.
https://www.mckinsey.com/capabilities/people-and-organizational-performance/our-insights/why-diversity-matters.

Kingma, Boris and Wouter van Marken Lichtenbelt, 2015. "Energy Consumption in Buildings and Female Thermal Demand." *Nature Climate Change* 5, 1054–1056.
https://www.nature.com/articles/nclimate2741.

Rick Seltzer, Rick. 2017. "The Slowly Diversifying Presidency." *Inside Higher ED*, June 20.
https://www.insidehighered.com/news/2017/06/20/college-presidents-diversifying-slowly-and-growing-older-study-finds.

Simon Caulkin, Simon. 2022. "Will Women Leaders Change the Future of Management?" *Financial Times*, April 2.
https://www.ft.com/content/6bf98d62-0ff4-4f19-a37d-e53f40abf6f2.

CHAPTER 11

Packard, Grant and Jonah Berger. 2021. "How Concrete Language Shapes Customer Satisfaction." *Journal of Consumer Research* 47. No. 5. 787-806.

Mehrabian, Albert. 1971. *Silent Messages* (1st ed.). Belmont, CA: Wadsworth Publishing Company.

Moore, Alex. 2016. "7 Tips for Getting More Responses to Your Emails." *Boomerang*, February 12.
https://blog.boomerangapp.com/2016/02/7-tips-for-getting-more-responses-to-your-emails-with-data.

Ring, Susannah. 2017. "The Confusing Way Mexicans Tell Time." *BBC Travel*, July 26. https://www.bbc.com/travel/article/20170725-the-confusing-way-mexicans-tell-time.

CHAPTER 12

Bean IV, Delcie. 2019. "A Small Tech Company Tried It All to Stop Employee Turnover." *CNBC Report*. December 3. https://www.cnbc.com/2019/12/03/a-tech-firm-tried-it-all-to-stop-turnover-only-one-thing-worked.html.

Kantor, Julie. 2017. "MentoringUP: Millennials Reverse Mentor at Pershing." *HuffPost*, July 6. https://www.huffpost.com/entry/mentoringup-millennials-reverse-mentor-at-pershing_b_59518180e4b0f078efd98420.

Meyers, Nancy. 2015. "THE INTERN," Movie Produced by Nancy Meyers.

Neff, Thomas and James Citrin. 2005. *You Are in Charge—Now What*. New York, NY: Three River Press.

CHAPTER 13

Epstein, David. 2019. *Range: Why Generalists Triumph in a Specialized World*. New York, NY: Riverhead Books.

Handscomb, Christopher and Shail Thaker, 2018, "Activate Agility: The Five Avenues to Success." *McKinsey Report*, February 1.

Hillenbrand, Philipp, Dieter Kiewell, Rory Miller-Cheevers, Ivan Ostojic, and Gisa Springer. 2019. "Traditional Company, New Business: The Paring That Can Ensure an Incumbent's Survival." *McKinsey Report*. https://www.mckinsey.com/industries/oil-and-gas/our-insights/traditional-company-new-businesses-the-pairing-that-can-ensure-an-incumbents-survival.

Hylton, Sara. 2021. "Veterans in the Labor Force: 6 Stats." US Department of Labor Blog, November 9. https://blog.dol.gov/2021/11/9/veterans-in-the-labor-force-6-stats.

CHAPTER 14

Breslin, Beau. 2021. A Constitution for The Living: Imaging How Five Generations of Americans Would Rewrite the Nations Fundamental Law. Stanford, CA: Stanford University Press.

Boutetiere, Hortense de la, Alberto Montagner, and Angelika Reich. 2018. "Unlocking Success in Digital Transformations." McKinsey Report. October 29.
https://www.mckinsey.com/capabilities/people-and-organizational-performance/our-insights/unlocking-success-in-digital-transformations.

Bucy, Michael, Adrian Finlayson, Greg Kelly, and Chris Moye. 2016. "The 'How' of Transformation." McKinsey Report, May 9. https://www.mckinsey.com/industries/retail/our-insights/the-how-of-transformation.

Condon, Mark. 2022. "We Asked 1000 Photographers What Camera They Use in 2022." Shotkit. October 2. https://shotkit.com/camera-survey.

Dannemiller, K. D., and R. W. Jacobs. 1992. "Changing the Way Organizations Change: A Revolution of Common Sense." The Journal of Applied Behavioral Science 28, no. 4, 480–498.

Dow, Jameon. 2021. "VW CEO Herbert Diess Invites Elon Musk to Talk on How Tesla Innovates Quickly." Electrek, October 16. https://electrek.co/2021/10/16/vw-ceo-herbert-diess-invites-elon-musk-to-talk-on-how-tesla-innovates-quickly.

Morris, Stephen. 2009. "Domino Chain Reaction (Geometric growth in action)," October 4. https://www.youtube.com/watch?v=y97rBdSYbkg.

CHAPTER 15

Arbulu, Roberto, Gary Fisher, and Jack Hartung. 2021. "Stage Gate - What Are the Implications?" Project Production Institute. https://projectproduction.org/journal/stage-gate-what-are-the-implications.

Citrin, James and Richard Smith. 2005. The 5 Patterns of Extraordinary Careers: The Guide for Achieving Success and Satisfaction. New York, NY: Crown Business.

Cooper, Robert. 1993. Winning at New Products: Accelerating the Process from Idea to Launch. Reading, MA: Perseus Books Publishing.

Nieto-Rodriguez, Antonio. 2021. "The Project Economy Has Arrived." Harvard Business Review, December. https://hbr.org/2021/11/the-project-economy-has-arrived.

Rapid Results Institute, 2022. " The Path to Change: 100-Day Challenges in Zacatecas' Criminal Justice System." https://www.rapidresults.org/blog/2021/3/4/tptc-zacatecas.

CHAPTER 16

Daxueconsulting, 2022. "The Future of Nike in China After Shutting Down Its Nike Run Club App in 2022." July 20. https://daxueconsulting.com/nike-in-china.

Delgado, Patricia. 2021. "Recruitment and Retention of Professional Hispanic Millennials: A Participatory Program Series for Organizational Leaders." PhD Dissertation. The University of Arizona.

Trompenaars, Fons. 1998. *Riding the Waves of Culture: Understanding Cultural Diversity in Business.* New York, NY: McGraw-Hill.

John, Leslie. 2021. "Savvy Self-Promotion." *Harvard Business Review,* May-June. https://hbr.org/2021/05/savvy-self-promotion.

Nike, 2021. "NIKE CEO John Donahoe on Q1 2022 Results - Earnings Call Transcript." *Seeking Alpha.* September 23. https://seekingalpha.com/article/4456830-nike-inc-s-nke-ceo-john-donahoe-on-q1-2022-results-earnings-call-transcript.

Robson, David. 2017. "How East and West Think in Profoundly Different Ways." *BBC report.* January 19. https://www.bbc.com/future/article/20170118-how-east-and-west-think-in-profoundly-different-ways.

Zhang, Longmei, Ray Brooks, Ding Ding, Haiyan Ding, Hui He, Jing Lu, and Rui C. Mano, 2018. "China's High Savings: Drivers, Prospects, and Policies." *International Monetary Fund,* WP/18/277. https://www.imf.org/en/Publications/WP/Issues/2018/12/11/Chinas-High-Savings-Drivers-Prospects-and-Policies-46437.

CHAPTER 17

Diamond, Jared. 2012. *The World Until Yesterday, What Can We Learn from Traditional Societies?* New York, NY: Penguin Books.

FAIL! Inspiring Resilience. 2019. "Amy Edondson: Failure's Mixed Bag." December 5. https://www.youtube.com/watch?v=VH9Y3-lCigM.

Goss, Nick. 2022. "Celtics' Ime Udoka Reveals Three Teams That Passed on Him for Head Coach Jobs." *NBC Sports.* May 31. https://www.nbcsports.com/boston/celtics/celtics-ime-udoka-re-veals-three-teams-passed-him-head-coach-jobs.

Hirotsu, Dennis. 2021. "Unleashing API Leadership Potential." *Internal Presentation at ExxonMobil ACE Meeting.*

McLaughlin, Eliott. 2015. "92-Year-Old Becomes Oldest Woman to Complete Marathon." *CNN News,* June 2. https://www.cnn.com/2015/06/01/us/san-diego-marathon-oldest-woman-finishes.

CHAPTER 18

Beheshti, Naz. 2019. "10 Timely Statistics About the Connection Between Employee Engagement and Wellness." *Forbes.* Jan 16. https://www.forbes.com/sites/nazbeheshti/2019/01/16/10-time-ly-statistics-about-the-connection-between-employee-engage-ment-and-wellness/?sh=5a9b2f2c22a0.

Sandvik, Jason, Richard Saouma, Nathan Seegert, and Christopher T. Stanton. 2022. "Why Your Mentoring Program Should Be Manda-tory." *Harvard Business Review.* September-October. https://hbr.org/2022/09/why-your-mentoring-pro-gram-should-be-mandatory.

Zhao, Xinjin. 2022. *Leadership Survey.* https://www.onbecomingaleader.net/survey.

APPENDIX B
ACKNOWLEDGMENT

―――

"Writing to me is an advanced and slow form of reading. If you find a book you really want to read but it hasn't been written yet, then you must write it." This a how Nobel Laureate Toni Morrison once said about writing a book.

I have never found something to be truer. I have read extensively about leadership over the years. Many of them inspired me to reflect and taught me about how to lead in a certain way. However, no one single book has truly answered my long quest for clarity on leadership. It may well be because of how the books were read, not necessarily how they were written.

With some encouragement and a little bit of blind faith, I committed to write this book as part of my continued quest for clarity on my own leadership journey. It has been a much bigger commitment than I had anticipated. At the same time, it has been a journey, even with all the labors and pains, that I have enjoyed much more than I expected.

At the beginning of this journey, I imagined that writing a book was going to be mostly an introspective activity. I was going to be locked in my office for several months and writing paragraph by paragraph, page by page, chapter by chapter, until I finish a manuscript. I was mentally prepared to have some lonely time for the project. With leadership being such a well-studied topic, I wondered how much new insights I really could offer that would be of value and interest to other aspiring leaders.

I did not truly appreciate what Professor Eric Koester said at the Creator Program: "never write alone." It turned out he was exactly right. It takes a village to write a book, and a writer does not have to know absolutely everything there is to know about a subject. I certainly do not.

On the one hand, the process is indeed introspective at times, and it forced me to reflect on the triumphs and struggles throughout my own leadership journey. However, writing the book gives me the privilege to connect with so many wonderful leaders or aspiring leaders, and brings new light to this profound subject that many struggle throughout their careers.

As I was progressing with the writing, I realized writing a book is not really about me or what I know. It is about the insights I could harvest and crystallize from the research, from reading, more importantly, from the conversations with many leaders who have generously agreed to share their leadership perspectives with me through interviews.

In addition, I also had the privilege of being connected with two hundred seventy thousand people around the world who subscribe to my weekly leadership blog. Engagements with them often provides unique inspiration to many of topics I am writing. I also want to thank the five hundred sixty people who participated in my leadership survey I developed solely for the purpose of this book. The survey results in many ways validated some of the hypotheses about leadership development I had, but also shed new lights beyond my original assumptions.

Ultimately, writing the book is really about what the readers can internalize and, as a result, take actions to develop a better appreciation of their leadership values and purposes on their leadership journey.

Although most of the concepts and frameworks are not necessarily new, being able to weave personal experiences of my own, or experiences shared by other leaders, makes the insights more compelling and relatable. In addition, the fact that leadership seems to be an ever-changing concept provides an opportunity for us to continue the exploration and quest.

Writing the book has benefited me deeply because it has allowed me to discover so much about myself. It helps me to gain a better appreciation on what really matters to me. It becomes a powerful way to get in touch with my values and motivations. I am hoping reading the book also catalyzes an infection point on the journey of your leadership quest as well.

Many have made this book possible. To the extent I can cite the names, I would like to acknowledge the following people who provided direct support for my book journey.

First of all, I want to thank all the people who have shared their leadership insights by agreeing to be interviewed for the book. Everyone has unique perspectives and insights and conversations with each of you have enriched my appreciation of different perspectives of leadership. Ultimately, those insights will benefit readers in the broad community. On behalf of all of the readers, thank you!

Clotilde Bouaoud, Jennie Byrne, Marisol Capellan, Phillip Dearing, Patricia Delgado-Peña, Grace Gong, Philip Hah, Rose Hall, Keith Hartsfield, Ananya Jain, Gary Kaplan, Yiying Lu, Tim Lynch, Scott McEntyre, David Olivencia, Deepti Pahwa, Jason Patent, Matt Poepsel, Mosa Rahimi, Ricardo Rosello, Laurence Smith, Jeremy Suard, Ilya Tabakh, Stephen Tang.

I especially would like to mention Rose Hall not only for the leadership insight about self-awareness in Chapter 3, but being a support for the book all along the way, Keith Hartsfield for sharing his personal leadership experience in China, Ricardo Rossello for sharing his leadership experience in a very open and insightful way as the former governor of Puerto Rico.

Second, the team of people from the Creator Institute and New Degree Press have been extremely supportive. Without their support, and also the necessary nudges to keep me accountable for my commitment when needed, I would never have been able to complete this book. While thanking Professor Eric Koester who originally convinced me to join the writing program, it took a wonderful community of many behind the scene to make the book a reality. Here is an incomplete list. Thank you all for your encouragement and support.

Amanda Brown (Copy Editing), Kera Ann Dawkins (Head of Community Support), Vladimir Dudaš (Layout Editor), Grant Gieseke (Revision Editor), Eric Koester (Founder of Creator Institute), Zach Marcum (Developmental Editor), Jacques Moolman (Marketing Advisor), Sherman Morrison, Lisa Patterson (Acquiring Editor), Gjorgji Pejkovski (Cover Design), Leah Pickett (Copy Editing), John Saunders, (Strategy Advisor), Mary Ann Tate (Structural Editor), Crystal Winters (Copy Editing).

I especially want to thank John Saunders for his early advice to conduct the leadership survey which became an important of the book.

In addition, I would like to thank the following beta readers who provided valuable feedbacks for the manuscript. Your feedbacks have made this a better book. I have been able to incorporate some, but not all of the suggestions. I will certainly consider all the suggestions again for future editions.

Francesco Benedetti, Rose Hall, Max Heinritz-Adrian, Sylvie Howard, Nan Li, Tim Lunch, Rika Nakazawa, Sonal Soveni, Feng Xiao.

I want to acknowledge all the people who supported me by pre-ordering my book during the pre-sale campaign period, which made the whole project possible. The direct financial support was sufficient to cover the cost of revision, copy editing, cover design, layout, and the initial printing. I certainly hope you will not only enjoy reading the book but also turn some of the insights into leadership actions. Since you will be the first group of people who actually read my book, I would love to hear your direct feedbacks about what you love about the book, as well as opportunities for making improvement for future editions.

Arunnambi Alagirisamy, Shahid Alam, Mohammed Alsabih, Erin Arms, David Ayrapetyan, Francesco Maria Benedetti, Nazeer Bhore, Svetlana Bouwens, Dan Brady, Richard Bren, Michael Brisch, Tanya Bryja, Eric Bunnelle, Natthorn C, Marisol Capellan, Carole M Carrion, Bridget Centenera, Weining Chang, Benoit des Ligneris, Lianne Detrick, Rumyana Dimova, Yanni Dong, Fred Doty, Sherry Ellmore, Nancy Feng, Sergio Fernandes, Anthony Fung, Sylvie Gallier Howard, Devin Gary, Franco Gentile, Malcolm Goodwin, Sripad Gopala, Rose Hall, Jenny Happas, Max Heinritz-Adrian, Sun Yee Ho, James Huggins, Jiajie Huo, Amrit Jalan, Sharon James, Angela Jones, Chuck Jones, Katherine Kalama, Haresh Keswani, Sang-Won Kim, Eric Koester, Borislava Kostova, Marjaana Laitila, Rohit Lall, Daisy Le, I-Mei Liao, Juan Lizama, Bo Lu, Amy Mahoney, Olando Marrero, Mark McCourt, Seamus McKeague , Shaojun Miao, Manickababu Muthu, Gary Nako, Cash Nashery, Olu Olaoye, Joanne Ooi, Jonathan Pelletier, Indra Permana, Rama Perubotla , Michael Pomianek, Huifeng Qian, jayakiran Rebelli, Bob Riley, Sam Ryu, Jenny Seagraves, Laszlo Seress, Polina Shishkina, David

Sibley, Colin Sng, Sonal Soveni, Samantha Straede, John Studdard, Ilya Tabakh, Stephen Tang, Elizabeth Rosebud Tetteh, Lok Tse, Chantal Unger, William Van Sweringen, Sridhara Venkateshaiah, Hongwei Wang, Erika Wilburn-Campbell, Rio Winardi, Rick Wormsbecher, Aisha Wyatt, Han Xia, Feng Xiao, Yun Yang, Gregory Yeo, Xiaohua Yi, Jison Zabala, Lei Zhang, Shuo Zhang, Yunlong Zhang, Daniel Zhao, David Zhao, Qun Zhao, Nan Zhou

I would like to specifically acknowledge the direct financial support from Francesco Maria Benedetti, Katherine Mizrahi Rodriguez, and Holden Lai, co-founders of Osmoses for their support and interest in my leadership book project. I also would like to thank Qun Zhao, a fellow Wharton graduate and Vice President of Wharton Shanghai Club who actively supported the pre-sale campaign of my book in China.

Finally, I would like to acknowledge the support from my wife, Luhong, for the endeavor. It would not have been possible to write this book as my first retirement project without her full support and understanding. In addition, my sons, Daniel and David, for their wholehearted support directly and indirectly. Both read my manuscript chapter by chapter and provided invaluable feedback to make the book a better one. I certainly hope they will also gain a few insights about leadership along the way, which might benefit them on their own journeys.

Thank you.